Rewire

Learning
Resources
Centre

Rewire

A Radical Approach to Tackling Diversity and Difference

Chris Yates and Pooja Sachdev

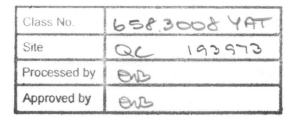

Bloomsbury Information
An imprint of Bloomsbury Publishing Plc

B L O O M S B U R Y

LONDON · OXFORD · NEW YORK · NEW DELHI · SYDNEY

Bloomsbury Information
An imprint of Bloomsbury Publishing Plc

50 Bedford Square	1385 Broadway
London	New York
WC1B 3DP	NY 10018
UK	USA

www.bloomsbury.com

BLOOMSBURY and the Diana logo are trademarks of Bloomsbury Publishing Plc

First published 2015

British Library Cataloguing-in-Publication Data
A catalogue record for this book is available from the British Library.

ISBN: PB: 978-1-4729-1398-2
ePDF: 978-1-4729-1400-2
ePub: 978-1-4729-1399-9

Library of Congress Cataloging-in-Publication Data
Yates, Chris (Human resources director), author.
Rewire : a radical approach to tackling diversity and difference / Chris Yates and Pooja Sachdev.
pages cm
ISBN 978-1-4729-1398-2 (hardback) – ISBN 978-1-4729-1399-9 (ebook) – ISBN 978-1-4729-1400-2 (epdf) 1. Diversity in the workplace. 2. Corporate culture. 3. Organizational behavior. I. Sachdev, Pooja. II. Title.
HF5549.5.M5Y38 2015
658.3008–dc23
2015018665

Typeset by Integra Software Services Pvt. Ltd.
Printed and bound by CPI Group (UK) Ltd, Croydon, CR0 4YY

In loving memory of Yoginder Mohan Sachdev
(23 Feb 1940–17 May 2015).

He was only seven years old when his family was forced
to leave everything they had and move across the border during
India's partition. He taught me that love, courage and character
are what make us who we are, not race or religion.

Contents

Acknowledgements

This book is the product of many years of working, thinking and learning. Countless conversations, experiences and coaching moments over our careers have brought us to this point. We are grateful to all the friends, family and colleagues who played a part in this journey, but there are a few people in particular we would like to mention and thank.

For inspiration, support and encouragement at different points in our careers: John Powell, Ann Almeida, Paul Riddell, Peter Glick, Simon Western, Hazel Spears, Christine Robinson, Gabriella Giglio and Kim Hauer.

For expertise and invaluable advice through the writing process: Alana Clogan, Rosie Bick and Stephen Rutt at Bloomsbury. We could not have asked for a better publisher to work with on this.

For generously giving time, and feedback on early drafts: Sophie Skinner, Gemma Harper, Jorge Aisa Dreyfus, Lynn O'Connor, Linda Chavis and Ritika Sachdev. You helped us bring this book to the finish line!

And finally, and most importantly, our families:

Rea: For the love, encouragement and belief. For keeping the family safe when I was absent and for picking me up when lost.

Elisabeth Yates: For the proofreading, direction and critical feedback at key moments and helping to keep the family sane.

Zen: For your love and patience, your line-by-line, honest critique and for bearing with me while I had my head buried in my laptop for hours and days on end. I could not have done this without you.

My parents, Priti and Yoginder Sachdev: For instilling in me, from the start, the passion and the courage to say what I think, and to whose home I eventually, naturally returned to finish this book. Dad, I wish you were here to read this.

Preface

Before we begin the book, we wanted to introduce ourselves. We hope this will help to set the scene and give you a picture of where we are coming from, as we describe some key life events that led up to us writing this book. We have intentionally written our stories separately (and in our own personal styles) so that you hear our distinct 'voices', which you will hear again throughout the book in the personal examples we relate.

Each of us has our unique background and life experiences that shape us, and form our ideas. These are our stories.

Pooja

I first became acutely aware of diversity and difference when I was 16 and had just started college. I went from Mumbai, India, where I grew up, to a small town in Wisconsin, USA; from an average annual temperature of 27.2°C (81°F) and a city with a population of 20.5 million to a town with a population of about 78,000 and an average annual snowfall of 48 inches! To say it was a culture shock would be an understatement. One of many international students grappling with the same issues, I found myself thrust into a world, which defined me primarily by the colour of my skin. Where previously I was defined by being someone's daughter or the girl who lives on 25th road or the school prefect, I was now, first and foremost, a representative of my entire nation. Suddenly, I found myself brushing up on my Hindi (unbelievably for many, English was the first language I learnt) and on my Bollywood trivia (it always surprised people when I didn't know about the latest movies, actors, songs – I was a bigger fan of English pop music like many other teenagers living in Mumbai). When India was in the news for something good, I felt a patriotic pride that I had never felt before. I was an Indian now. Ironically, it took moving out of India to the other side of the world to realize this.

And just when I was getting comfortable in my new expanded identity of being an Indian and an American college student at the same time, I moved again, this time to the UK. Now it was even more difficult to answer the simple question people always ask when they first meet you: 'Where are you from?'. My answer would depend on where I was and who I was talking to. In India, I was from London, and in London I was either from the States or India. I was never from the place I actually was in! It took a few years before I began to see this as an interesting complexity rather than an unsettling one.

Naturally, these transitions have brought up lots of questions for my inquisitive, liberal arts–educated, international mind. What is it that forms our identities and gives us a sense of pride and belonging? How do I define 'my groups' that I identify with, in what ways do I feel the same as others and in what ways different? How do ideas of sameness and difference play a role in my interactions, relationships, life choices and aspirations? Twenty-odd years and two master's degrees later, I am still asking the same questions.

As I write this, I am watching my eleven-month-old daughter trying to destroy a toy truck by taking various bits apart and banging it on the floor repeatedly while I, the broken record, say repeatedly 'gently, baby' and 'play nicely'. I recall how my brother's transformer was my favourite toy as a child and I relished taking it apart! I wonder how much of who we are and what we believe comes from within and how much comes from the outside. Are men and women essentially all that different or is it the messages we are given – to be tough or to play gently?

Gender differences have never been so prominent in my life as now. Having recently given birth, I am settling in to my role as a new mum and connecting in a whole new way with other women. My professional life seems a distant memory as I cope with sleepless nights and constant cooking, cleaning and feeding. Of course the heartbreakingly beautiful moments with my daughter – like that first giggle! – that intersperse these tasks make it all worthwhile. I am grateful for her and for being able to be with her during these precious months. Yet at the back of my mind is the firm belief that this is temporary and that I will return to 'real work' soon. In fact, I am not even going to 'waste' the time at home and so I am actually writing a book while she naps in the afternoons!

People have said that raising a child is the hardest and the most rewarding thing you can do. I can see that now, more clearly than ever before. And yet, it is not enough for me to do it exclusively. Why? Because hidden in the depths of my mind is a script which I have learnt which tells me that I would not be good enough or living up to my potential enough if 'all' I did was raise a child. I feel ashamed to say it out loud because I firmly believe that underestimation of the importance of childcare is the root of so many gender inequalities in our society and our organizations. Yet my scripts are so powerful that despite knowing it is irrational, I would never be happy, or fully fulfilled, if I didn't go back to paid work and 'do something' with my life.

We all have our scripts. Most of them are rooted in what we heard our parents say – to be tough or play gently. Or to make money, or work hard. Some of our scripts are gendered and some are culturally based. When our scripts clash with scripts of other genders and other cultures, or with contradictory life experiences, we have to dig really deep to uncover where they come from, whether they still apply and what we will keep and what we will discard.

So it is with organizations. All organizations have a history – how they started and where and how they grew can often explain why things are done the way they are today. Yet a lot of organizational practices remain unchallenged. And rather than adapting organizational scripts to evolving needs and circumstances, the scripts can sometimes be debilitating. In this book, I hope we will inspire you to unearth your personal and your organizational scripts and challenge them. Not just as a one-off exercise but constantly keeping vigil on where our intentions, processes, values, decisions, structures and stories are coming from and what they are achieving. I feel this wider vision of ourselves and our structures alone can open up the possibility of being truly diverse, equal, inclusive and the best we can be.

Chris

I was born in the 1960s in London. I grew up with my grandparents in Guyana. I returned back to London for my early teen years and then onto a worldwide tour of life that has seen me work and live in every continent.

I share two personal stories that capture how we (I) are programmed through our earliest experiences.

Growing up, I was flooded with images from the media of Americans living in the 'South' who love guns and hunting and who were associated with the Ku Klux Klan. It signified people who typically hate anyone black. Films such as *Mississippi Burning, Roots, To Kill a Mocking Bird, Gone with the Wind* and most recently *Django Uncovered* all tell the story (and history) of a group of people who live outside of the cities in the middle and south of the United States of America who are likely to lynch me, hate me and who should be treated with extreme caution. Everything I saw in the media and heard in the stories told me to fear them.

In 2013, I moved to the mid-west of America. I was invited to join a colleague on a hunting excursion, so after work one evening, I went to a hunting store to purchase a hunting bow. As I pulled up in the car park, my heart beat faster. The majority of the cars were pick-up trucks. Most of the pick-up trucks had National Rifle Association stickers on them and some strong anti-Obama sentiments displayed in strong language. These seemed to be the people that the mass media have 'trained' me to see as most likely in the world to hate me. Fear kicked in. I started thinking I could get lynched, my family would never see me again and I would be unlikely to get any justice as the local authorities were most likely to be friends or relatives of the owners of the pick-up trucks – this is what started running through my mind. The butterflies in my stomach were at a rave. My mouth went dry, and my muscles stiffened. Subconsciously I was already poised and ready to defend myself from extreme prejudice. This was fright, fight, FLIGHT system in full action. For those of you unfamiliar with this psychology model, when under threat, our bodies divert blood from our digestive system to the muscles in our arms and legs and to our brain. The purpose is that faced with threat, we are evolved to react quickly and be responsive to stay alive. This reaction triggers unconsciously and in the fraction of a second. In this case it was triggered by unconscious prejudice towards a section of white Americans who have been portrayed in the media in a particular way, but of whom I had had no previous real experience.

The staff and people I encountered in the store – after I mastered my own prejudice and walked in – were among the nicest, most friendly people one could hope to meet. They were helpful, welcoming and smiling. I made instant friends. If I had listened to my gut reaction that day, I would have turned around and left, and my prejudice would have remained intact.

Going further back in my life, as a teenager in West London in the 1980s, I recall a similar experience. I grew up having an image of Chelsea Football Club fans as Neo-Nazis, skinheads and people who are violent towards ethnic minorities. At a new job, one day, I was invited to the executive floor to meet one of the board members. He has a coffee mug with a Chelsea Football Club emblem. Again, similar to the hunting shop car park, my stomach started churning. The executive was balding, well built, and seemed to be about the right age to have been 'active' as a 1980s football hooligan. Am I to suppose that this board executive of an FT 100 company was once chasing people who looked like me down a side street shouting racist slogans? He smiled. I smiled, while actively trying to control the ideas that were going through my mind about who he is likely to be and more importantly how he is likely to treat me. At one point in my life having the reaction to emblem of a football club was useful. It nudged me to run instead of walk, be sharp and quick-witted and fast of foot on the public transport systems of London – but that was in the 1980s. In this corporate environment today, it blocks my ability to be open and fully attentive to my executive colleague. He turns out to be one of my biggest sponsors and a good friend.

My instinctive fear of who I see as 'others' could one day have saved my life. But today, it could have cut out an important and positive experience from my life.

Fear of difference both protects us – and is sensible sometimes – and yet blocks us. Propaganda creates fear and sometimes stops us from experiencing each other as individuals. Propaganda can work the other way – to steer us to be more open to others and to counter stereotypical images.

There has been much talk in recent years in the industry of Diversity and Inclusion about unconscious bias. The example above is an example of my own bias, which came into operation as I drove into that car park. Unfortunately, there has been relatively little talk about what to do about this phenomenon – how it can be controlled, mastered, managed and directed for the good of society as a whole.

Examining societal collective experience and drawing on ideas from sociology, psychology, religion, mythology and neurophysiology, we can learn so much about how we as humans build personal under-standing and culture.

While seeking an answer to how to tackle this peculiar problem of sustainable culture change I was directed by my mother-in-law to John Powell, a former professor at Ohio State University, now at Berkeley, who had studied this area. When I met him for dinner I asked him for a silver bullet – a simple way to pierce the very heart of the issue. John told me that the silver bullet that I was looking for was 'propaganda'. I hope that this book will show you that propaganda is absolutely the right starting place. And why.

Section 1

Introduction

Chapter 1

What this book is about

Chapter Outline

Why we wrote this book

This book was born out of frustration. We have worked in the area of diversity and inclusion, in some form, for most of our careers and over this time, we have found ourselves having the same tired conversations and doing the same things in different organizations, with little significant change being seen. Organizations are obsessed with benchmarking themselves against others, and the awards industry drives endless attempts to copy and replicate what is seen to be 'best practice' – but very few new ideas emerge from this. Small shifts in percentages of women or minorities, or successful execution of programmes like mentoring or development days, are celebrated, but on the whole, things don't seem to have changed much.

We wanted to break out of this stagnation by really re-thinking this area of work. We felt it was time to make a fundamental shift in how we understand and tackle diversity. We wanted to find a radically new approach.

We started by working and talking with a wide range of organizations across different sectors and in different countries to find out how they define and deal with diversity. We wanted to understand what has worked and what hasn't worked, and why. We spoke with senior leaders, junior employees, consultants, experts and specialists from some of the world's most prominent global organizations and posed the question: What's stopping us from seeing real progress in this area?

We heard many of the 'usual' answers such as gender differences, lack of flexible working, childcare demands, and the role of bias. We heard of some issues that were unique to a particular organization or country or industry, for example the nature of the work in mining, or the historic issue of caste in India. However, regardless of what type of organization it is and where it is coming from, one theme always emerges: the role of culture. We heard countless remarks along the lines of '*we have the policies in place but the mindset of people hasn't changed*' or '*that's just the way things work around here*'. This naturally led us to ask: if we know that diversity is essentially about culture, why aren't Diversity and Inclusion specialists doing more to address culture?

The big idea

The key message of this book is this: in order to create significant and sustainable shifts in diversity and inclusion, we need to look at it not as an HR issue but as a human issue, rooted in culture. We need to move away from a narrow process approach and take a new, holistic perspective that addresses culture – both organizational and social culture.

One evening, I am in a cab riding home and we pass a Muslim family who are walking in the street. The driver (who is white) references them, '… bloody foreigners, if they don't like our way of life they should go back where they came from'. I am a bit taken aback because like the Muslim family we passed, I have brown skin, and my parents were immigrants. I can't understand how he thinks it is OK to say this in my presence, so I ask. His response is that I am not a foreigner because 'my lot' (I take it he means British West Indians) have been in the UK for a long time, that we speak the lingo (English, in my case with a London accent), we eat the same food, worship the same God, listen to the same music, have the 'same values' and 'your lot' fought in the war with 'my lot'.

He sees me as part of his group because he chooses to focus on the aspects that make us the same. He sees the Muslim family as part of an 'other' because he chooses to focus on difference – in religion, dress or custom – even though I potentially might have more in common with the Muslim family.

Before we can understand how to deal with diversity and difference at work, we have to understand the wider context of how we draw the lines around who we see as 'us' and who we see as 'other'. The choices we make about where we draw these lines determines how we see ourselves and how we treat others, and this lies at the heart of diversity.

Society dictates much of how we group ourselves and what associations we make, as does our personal experience and background. These lines of demarcation are contextual and constantly shifting, and yet they are powerful. They create feelings of sameness or difference, and drive either acceptance, tolerance and empathy *or* contempt, competition and conflict between people.

Culture – organizational and societal – serves to create and reinforce these categorizations and world views, which ultimately drive (or detract from) equality and inclusion.

Organizational and social cultures

We know from other aspects of organizational functioning that in order to embed changes in any aspect – be they technological advancements or mergers/acquisitions or geographical changes – they must be accompanied by a consideration of organizational culture. Yet, efforts in the area of diversity and inclusion often ignore culture, and focus only on addressing the 'symptoms' of the problem through, for instance, quotas or new policy documents or sponsored social activity for women or minorities.

We also operate in a wider social context where we are influenced by national culture, politics, religion and tradition. The inequality between men and women, for example, extends beyond the workplace. We cannot ignore the wider societal bias (and in many contexts, outright violence) against women that exists in most cultures, where traditional female roles are less empowered than male roles, and women have far fewer opportunities available to them. Society impacts what happens inside organizations. And organizations also have the opportunity to change society.

An Organizational Development approach to diversity

We draw on the field of Organizational Development (OD). This is an area of work that deals in understanding and changing culture. We therefore refer to taking an 'OD Approach' to diversity. This means that we take a holistic and humanistic view of the organization, not just a process or mechanistic view. The organization is seen as a system, an ever-changing organism that flourishes when its individual parts are aligned.

The approach we outline in this book leans heavily on principles from this discipline. It is a comprehensive approach, which takes into account how cultures form and change. We use this approach to identify what aspects of culture need to be examined or changed to support our goals of diversity, and how these changes can be brought about.

Why is this radical?

While the ideas, theories and techniques covered by this book are not brand new or revolutionary, we still call the approach radical. This is for two reasons, based on two meanings of the word[1]: 'an extreme change from traditional form' and 'going to the root or origin'.

1. *An extreme change from traditional form*:

    While the issue of culture and culture change in itself is not new, this is a new way of looking at diversity and inclusion. Normally diversity and inclusion have been dealt with through a narrow, process approach of 'fixing' the problem. In this book, we rethink this and challenge some of the prevailing current approaches.

    For example, we ask: why do current approaches continue to focus on single strands of difference like age, gender or ethnicity, when we all have complex multi-dimensional identities? And why do current approaches continue to focus heavily on numbers and metrics when it is behaviours that need to be examined?

We shift the *focus* radically: to look away from 'diversity' per se, and focus on something wider and more systemic: culture.

We also shift the *approach* radically: rather than looking at how to 'fix' the problem, we seek to intentionally create a new type of environment that is based on a collective, positive aspiration.

2. *Going to the root or origin*:

In order to look at and change culture, it is necessary to go back to basics and examine ourselves, our institutions and our assumptions. We need to look at our personal history, our organizational history and all the internal and external factors that influence us, and ultimately drive behaviour and culture.

We need to unpack why things are the way they are and what we can do to fundamentally 'rewire' ourselves differently.

Who should read this book?

The book is about diversity and inclusion at work but it is not intended to be a resource only for Diversity and Inclusion or HR professionals. Anyone who is interested in creating a more inclusive environment within an organization or in wider society may find this book interesting and valuable. It is written from an OD perspective, but should be applicable and accessible to not only OD practitioners but anyone who is acting as a consultant (internally or externally) for an organization or is part of a group that is interested in creating a sustainable values-based culture.

While difference and diversity is the focus, the approach outlined in this book is applicable to wider change efforts and the core method may be used in a variety of contexts to create cultural shifts.

The book simultaneously draws on theory and practice, and the ideas are illustrated using anecdotes from the authors' own personal and professional lives to bring out key messages. It is grounded in evidence from social sciences and from years of practice and experience in what works in personal and organizational change. The approach is outlined as an iterative, step-by-step method with practical guidance and examples at every stage. It has been tried and tested in different contexts and can be adapted to fit with the specific contextual requirements of any group.

How the book is structured

The book is in four sections as follows:

Section 1

In the first section, we discuss why we feel this work is so critical, why efforts so far have led to little change and what role organizations can and do play in approaching diversity more effectively and holistically.

Section 2

In the second section, we outline a *causal map*. This is a holistic depiction of the social and psychological factors that influence how individuals and organizations think, act and make decisions. It is these decisions and actions that ultimately influence how cultures form. The causal map forms a diagnostic framework for understanding how diversity and inclusion plays out in organizations.

Section 3

In the third section, we draw on theories from the causal map to outline a new, tactical approach for creating a diverse and inclusive culture based on OD principles. Six steps are outlined in an *iterative approach* to culture change. By iterative, here, we mean that each step follows on from the last.

Section 4

In the final section, we discuss the potential for organizations to step forward and lead in this area with examples and reflections about the impact of organizational citizenship on shaping our world. We encourage you the reader to take the first steps in building a stronger and more inclusive society, wherever you are based.

---

[1] http://dictionary.reference.com/browse/radical?s=t, Retrieved 10 January 2014.

Chapter 2

A critique of current approaches

Chapter Outline

What drives diversity efforts

There are three broad reasons for organizations to be interested in diversity and inclusion:

- MUST
- SHOULD
- WANT

The 'must' is driven by equality legislation and rules set by governing organizations and industry bodies. The aim is to avoid penalties, including payouts and negative publicity. Where this is the strongest or only motivator, diversity efforts tend to 'tick the boxes' and do the bare minimum needed. Diversity initiatives in this context are often an 'add on', and sometimes even an impediment to normal organizational functioning.

The 'should' is the moral perspective. Fairness is seen as a universal virtue to strive for, so embracing diversity and being fair to all is the right thing to do. This assumes a uniform moral code among all within an organization, and a similar interpretation of 'how' to do the right thing and what is fair. In reality, this does not always exist at all levels and in all contexts. In fact, we know that prejudice and bias often exists at the unconscious level, so people may be unaware of their discriminatory attitudes and behaviours.

The 'want' comes from seeing diversity as a business benefit. This is often assumed to be the strongest motivator for those sitting at the top of organizations, making decisions about where to spend limited budgets, particularly in economically challenging times. It implies having a business case for diversity.

The business case debate

These are some of the strong theoretical arguments in support of the business case for diversity:

- *Widest possible talent pool*: having bias-free recruitment means the organization opens itself to the best available talent (regardless of where it comes from)
- *Innovation*: having a wider range of perspectives at the table can lead to fresh thinking and can enhance decision-making and creativity
- *Agility*: a diverse workforce leads to greater flexibility and adaptability as it creates more options for ways of thinking, communicating and working
- *Reflecting the customer base or the population*: a diverse organization will have an insight into the needs of people from different backgrounds and market/serve all potential customers
- *Employee engagement/productivity*: if employers demonstrate that they value employees from all backgrounds, it encourages people to be themselves and be more engaged
- *Cost*: the potentially financial cost of not managing diversity and difference properly – for example, conflict, failed mergers, tribunals, penalties, negative publicity and brand erosion

For many organizations, these theoretical arguments are not sufficient and statistical evidence is sought.

Many studies show statistical evidence for links between diversity/inclusion and business performance. Catalyst, a non-profit organization dedicated to gender equality in the workplace, reports that companies with a higher proportion of women on their boards earned a higher return on their invested capital, as well as sales.[1] Another report by McKinsey and Co.[2] showed that among European companies, those who had women on their board had a faster share growth than those who did not.

These reports demonstrate a link between gender diversity and the bottom line. Yet, often, even these are not seen to be sufficient. In almost every large organization, at any given time, someone in the 'diversity' team is always working on research for the business case: it is an *ongoing* agenda item! Executives are typically not easily convinced by correlational theoretical arguments so studies are often dismissed as irrelevant.

A question that always comes up for us when people talk about the 'business case' is: Why do we need a justification for equality? Do we need research to help us explain why we should be fair, regardless of financial implications? Fairness and equality for all *is a benefit in itself*. Moral perspective aside, is a clear-cut, simple commercial causal link even possible to demonstrate? First and foremost, how do we define the terms?

What do we mean by diversity and how do we measure success?

Diversity refers to a mix: differences in gender, ethnicity, ability, sexual orientation, faith, age, height, weight, etc. To 'measure' diversity, we might look at percentages of such groups present in the organization or in a particular team. The aim is generally to reflect the groups from the wider population within our organization. In order to check if this is happening, most organizations measure demographic data (e.g. the percentage of women/ethnic minorities/different age groups) in the organization and compare this with the percentages prevalent in the local population. Whether any particular groups are not represented or underrepresented within the organization prompts us to question why this may be the case.

Equality is shorthand for equal opportunities. It is about trying to ensure that no particular groups or people are unfairly disadvantaged in an organization – whether intentionally or unintentionally. It is about reviewing everyday processes and procedures to make sure that the way they are set up doesn't adversely impact a particular group or limit their opportunity to do well.

The terms 'equality' and 'diversity' are often used together or interchangeably. The assumption is that having equal opportunities naturally leads to diversity – for example if recruitment processes are fair, that means men and women have an equal chance of being selected. It's like flipping a coin. Diversity 'falls out' when opportunity is truly equal.

Equality and diversity don't always go hand in hand in this superficial way. For example, in order to fix past inequalities, quotas are sometimes set for underrepresented groups. On the surface, this is differential treatment, but the goal is to restore equality. This means that employers can take actions that help to encourage people from underrepresented groups to apply for a job or to improve their chances of success.

Are affirmative and positive actions 'equal' on the surface? No, on the surface, they are about treating one group more favourably than the other but the goal is to create long-term equality, and to level a previously unequal playing field. So when we refer to equal opportunities, it is not always about immediately giving all groups the *same* opportunities – it may sometimes play out in a way that does not look equal in the short term but is intended to create an overall, long-term equality.

So when you are trying to build a business case for diversity, what definitions do you adopt? Many simple attempts look at the effect of diversity literally; that is are more mixed teams (or organizations) more productive/successful/effective? This is too narrow an approach. Diversity in itself doesn't always necessarily improve team functioning. In fact, on the surface of it, homogenous teams might often appear to work more smoothly and make decisions faster (though they may not be the 'best' or most creative decisions). Just throwing people from different backgrounds together will not necessarily improve performance, and might even hinder it. People are naturally inclined to like, trust and protect the interests of those who are similar to themselves.

Inclusion is a broader term, more popular recently. It refers to how diversity plays out and how it is managed. It is about how much people feel included and part of something. How people see the culture and context of where they work has a very real and crucial impact on how they perform and what decisions they make.

Equality, diversity and inclusion are related concepts and they interact in different ways depending on the organization's operating context, its labour market, its wider social positioning and the actions, philosophies and strategies employed by those in power within it.

That leads, of course, to the other side of building a business case: **how we measure success**.

When we refer to business benefits, we often forget to stop and ask: 'who' benefits? Is it the employees of the organization, the senior management team, the shareholders or the general public? 'Organizational' benefits can vary, and there are a number of stakeholders whose interests can be taken into account – internal and external. In most pursuits of the business case, only internal measures of success are used – usually just profit or sales, and sometimes, employee engagement, staff retention and customer satisfaction.

However, the world external to the organization (communities, the economy) is also often affected by an organization's actions, even if the organization is a private enterprise, and this is often overlooked. Many large, multinational organizations today hold immense power to influence politics and the economy, and as such they also have a great responsibility for their impact on the world and people.

Traditionally, the private sector has focused on profits or sales as a key outcome measure, whereas the public sector has focused on social outcomes. To what extent should external indicators of success be included into the way 'business benefits' are defined in the private sector? Such questions are rarely asked, and the business case remains elusive because there is a widespread preference for simple, causal, linear, quantitative data in organizations, which is not only difficult to achieve, but also fails to capture the wider cultural and qualitative factors at play.

We continue to pursue simple linkages between 'diversity' and 'profit', which are susceptible to criticism on a number of grounds. There is the age-old debate about the *direction of causality*. Does diversity LEAD to business success or do successful companies attract a diverse workforce? You could argue that companies that are already successful have the money and resources to spend on diversity efforts and inclusive hiring. And that is why you see a link between diversity and profit, not because diversity leads to profit.

$$Diversity \rightarrow Profit$$
$$OR$$
$$Profit \rightarrow Diversity$$

In many such attempts, where quantitative data is analysed in the hope of finding a co-relation between one specific measure of diversity, and a valued output, such as sales performance, there is always some degree of subjectivity in how the finding is interpreted, what sense is made of the data, how they are then translated into actions (or not!).

For example, one large financial services organization decided to carry out a study on the effectiveness of all male versus mixed male-female teams. The Diversity and Inclusion team wanted to show that diverse teams were more effective. To their surprise, the results showed no significant difference. After some deliberation, they came forward with an explanation: they said that the teams that had been studied were comprised of senior employees. And at this level, they said, there is no difference because by this stage in their careers, women 'think like men'. This was a plausible explanation for many in the business but for others, it was evidence that money being invested in enhancing gender diversity at senior levels was not financially justified. You could argue it either way. And this led to yet another stalemate in the pursuit of linkage evidence.

In reality, it is not so simple and it is not so linear.

Diversity and profit are two variables in a complex equation where other factors play a mediating part, such as employee engagement and customer satisfaction. For example, a diverse and inclusive work environment makes employees feel more valued and engaged, and they then provide a better service to customers, which improves profit. So the relationship between diversity and profit may not be direct.

Furthermore, a wide range of external forces also affect the relationship between diversity and profit, including economics, politics, societal roles and norms, the nature of the industry, the nature of the work itself and the kind of management and leadership.

In seeking a simple linkage between diversity and profit, we fail to pursue a more rigorous and broader understanding of what aspects of diversity and inclusion affect what aspects of performance and how, and what other factors play a role.

Why current practices have failed to create much change

Short-term thinking and lack of strategy

A wide range of initiatives are considered to be part of the suite of 'diversity practices' today – from monitoring, quotas and target-setting to mentoring, reverse mentoring, sponsorship, affinity groups, bias training and targeted development programmes. All these practices have value, and can be effective. The problem, however, is that the intention is often driven by short-term thinking about how to *fix* a problem, rather than taking into account the whole picture and context.

Many organizations fail to take sufficient account of the 'how' along with the 'what' to do, and these practices take place randomly, without a plan – looking something like the image below.

It is important to have an overarching strategy to guide how these programmes are implemented; otherwise they end up being fragmented, tokenistic and disparate, thus losing their ability to create sustainable change. When used in a strategic way, the same strategies can have a much greater impact.

One of the reasons for this is that these efforts are driven by short-term goals, rather than a long-term strategy.

In most organizations, managers and leaders are expected to demonstrate short-term results. As a result, quick wins are favoured over long-term sustainable solutions. They continue to be driven by the linear business case, and the end-goal remains 'diversity' itself, rather than the wider organizational or social outcomes. So when that manager or leader or president moves on, things go back to how they were, and the organization (and society) remains stuck in a loop. On a social level, there is a similar pattern. Policy is driven by the dominant ideology – the political party that is in power and what their priorities are. This plays out, not only at the community and country level, but also influences how we think and react as organizations and individuals. When the political party changes, so do the diversity practices. Therefore, there is a lack of long-term, deliberate and cohesive action over time.

Influence and power

What approaches are chosen can often be a matter of who is choosing, rather than what the best choice is. Organizations are not democracies, and most decisions are ultimately based on the personal preferences of the few who are in power. Although the few at the top of an organization may indeed be highly experienced and qualified, they are human and not without personal bias. Their decisions may not always reflect what is best for the organization as a whole, even though they may claim to be working on behalf of shareholders or customers. Often, decisions made in organizations today reflect the legacy and principles of the original founders (the 'way things have always been done'), without enough attention being paid to the current context.

One recent survey of 863 board members of publicly traded companies in the United States by PricewaterhouseCoopers,[3] a professional services firm, showed that just 32 per cent of directors said that it is very important to have women on boards – so presumably, the rest did not consider gender diversity at senior levels to be very important. The percentage that thought racial diversity on boards was very important was even less – a mere 24 per cent. This may well be the single biggest reason we have not seen much change on this front, despite decades of work in diversity.

In most organizations, the powerful few at the top who are making decisions are mostly from dominant social groups rather than traditionally disadvantaged groups. These groups are less likely to experience negative discrimination in wider society and as such, they are said to hold more social power. This is not to say that people from these groups are more power-hungry or that people who are from other groups cannot be powerful. What it means is that they are less likely to have experienced, personally, the negative impact of social inequality, and therefore will presumably be less motivated *on a personal level* to change the status quo.

Who does diversity?

More often than not, the person appointed as the Head of Diversity in an organization comes from a minority, underrepresented or historically disadvantaged group. This is because a member of one of these groups will presumably (though not necessarily) be most passionate and most motivated to change things, but they are also likely to have less power or technical knowledge to do so, because of social and organizational inequalities already inherent in the system. So, they are given the (often tokenistic) responsibility for making changes but not the power to do so, thereby being predisposed to fail, or at least to struggle disproportionately in their efforts.

The role of HR: Poacher-turned-gamekeeper

Diversity also usually sits within the remit of HR departments. Traditionally, the role of HR has been largely bureaucratic and administrative - the original purpose of HR was to maintain employee relations, and monitor personnel processes (recruitment, training, dismissals, tribunals, health and safety, etc.) while ensuring that workplace legislation was being adhered to. This is a crucial role, as bureaucratic administrations are required to maintain effective operation of any organization or society.

In recent years, the role of HR has expanded to include more strategic and consultancy elements. However, traditional ways of working still influence how most issues are tackled. There is saying that when you have (or are) a hammer, everything you see is a nail. Well-meaning HR functions often use the same processes to tackle a wide variety of issues, and this includes Diversity & Inclusion. As a result, in many organizations, diversity is treated with a 'process' approach rather than a strategic and multidisciplinary one.

Beyond their traditional strength in administration, HR teams often play an involuntary role as a safeguard or protector of the organization from risk (change). Many HR processes are set up to maintain the status quo. Often HR is seen as, and indeed is, the branch of the organization that enforces the will of the management upon the organization. This is a difficult role, a conflict of interest, in both being the advocate for change and protecting the organization from change through process administration. One cannot successfully be both poacher and gamekeeper.

Cultural variations

In most multinational organizations headquartered in Europe or North America, the approach taken by central HR departments still tends to be Western-centric. Although this is slowly changing, very few organizations take adequate account of global cultural differences in their approach. This is not to say that the core principles of the organization should vary by geography, but when implementing the same principles in different parts of the world, cultural context should be taken into account so what is implemented is relevant and useful.

For example, childcare. This issue is central in Diversity & Inclusion (D&I) in the West – lack of suitable alternative childcare is a key barrier for parents (mainly mothers) returning to work after having children. However, in many collectivist cultures, such as India, where people live in 'joint families' or near relatives, another (often bigger) issue is elder-care – taking care of aging parents, who usually live at home either alone or with their children (rarely in care homes). Thus, while the principles of equality and diversity remain fairly universal, there are variations in how these play out in different cultural contexts, and these differences are not always taken into account.

Exclusionary rhetoric

There is also something generally limiting about the practice of Diversity and Inclusion being based on particular categories of difference such as gender, race and age. While it is important to identify historically disadvantaged groups so due attention can be paid to restoring the balance, the rhetoric of equality 'strands' itself can end up being exclusive. Often, what happens is that what we can easily see, measure and articulate gets attention and the rest gets missed. If we don't have enough data on sexual orientation or religion, for example (say, because we don't ask the question or not enough employees answer the question), these strands are given less priority, even though these are significant aspects of our identity.

I've always felt a little uncomfortable in employee networks, or employee 'resource groups' as they are sometimes referred to. I find myself wondering how much I have in common with the people around me. In a women's group, for example, we may all be female but we come from vastly different backgrounds – we come from different countries, different classes and we are of very different ages and appearances. We do share our gender, and yes, there are some issues that affect women as a whole (and don't affect men), but I don't personally feel that there are enough such issues that are so general that they apply to all of us in the same way. When I'm in the women's group, my gender identity is artificially highlighted, and I find myself suppressing my racial, religious and other identities. No single-stranded group like this can ever give me the opportunity to really be my 'whole self' because they are not set up to accept and understand the complex multistranded identity I bring. In some ways, they actually create more artificial lines, categories and divisions, and are exclusionary in their own way.

Diversity practice is usually designed around some key strands of difference. Generally these are gender, race and age, and in some cases, specific attention is also paid to aspects like religion, sexual orientation and marital status. Yet, there are millions of other ways in which we can discriminate against each other unjustifiably – height, for example, or weight or appearance. Particularly for men, several studies and surveys have found that being taller is associated with having a greater likelihood of being selected for jobs (even where the jobs have nothing to do with physicality), and that taller men, on average, earn more. The vast majority of CEOs are above average height and in most cultures, being tall is also associated with physical attractiveness, so taller men and more likely to find partners and have children. Many organizations ask to see pictures of potential candidates (easily done with Google and Facebook these days!), even if appearance is not a relevant job criterion. No attention is paid to how these pictures might skew their judgement because they may be biased towards people with a certain appearance.

Diversity is not just about black and white (as it is sometimes perceived to be) but about the subtle, biased, human ways in which we *all* think and act, and how we can become more aware of these so that we make better decisions, and make our societies more equal, and effective.

The problem with meritocracy

Many organizations now have adopted the word 'meritocracy' as a cultural aspiration to drive diversity. This, to some extent, addresses the limitation of focus on specific strands, and it is a useful, overarching concept to tie together diversity initiatives on a single guiding principle. However, it is not without problems.

Meritocracy is a philosophical idea, which states that people should be given power and opportunity to progress only on the basis of their 'merit'. On the surface, it makes sense and seems like an intuitively fair approach – to be blind to other aspects (such as age, appearance, gender, status, relationship), and just to focus on the person's talent. The reality is not so simple. We have seen many examples where despite having mertitocratic aims and processes, organizations do not really achieve meritocratic outcomes. We need to think below the surface to understand what is really happening. What are the invisible internal and external processes that are causing this disparity between organizational stated values and reality.

In fact, research[4] found that where organizations state explicit meritocratic goals, managers were actually *more* likely to favour male employees over (equally qualified) female employees when making reward decisions! Paradoxically, having the 'right' policies and rules in place can sometimes provide people with a shield behind which to hide, a defence. It gives organizations a veneer of doing the right thing even when it is not. Bureaucracy can exacerbate this paradox because people become solely responsible for the tasks such as filling the right forms, and not for the essential decisions.

In reality, a pure meritocracy is a myth. As human beings, we have inevitably different and limited views of the world. Peer reviews and performance appraisals are subjective tools that are often used as part of a 'meritocratic' process of judging someone, but they can never be completely free of bias.

Given this, and taking into account the wider context of socio-economic inequality that organizations ultimately reside in, claiming to be meritocratic is a red herring that can do more harm than good.

Political and philosophical basis

One of the broader reasons that diversity is not currently seen as being relevant to everybody is its philosophical and political basis.

Current approaches to diversity are seen to be based in a particular philosophy located in 'liberal' politics. Diversity practice originates in the utopic idea of equal opportunities and multiculturalism that is seen to be a left wing belief. As such, it is vulnerable to attack from the right wing and becomes the subject of party politics and personal or corporate ideology rather than being seen as a core value (and commercial necessity).

We need to reframe the issue as one that is universal and neutral, one that affects us all. It should be seen to be a part of human rights, because everyone has at least one aspect of our identity which, at some point of time, will either be in the minority somewhere or disadvantaged unjustifiably – whether it is one of the 'main strands' in equality politics (age, gender, race, etc.) or another aspect (such as our appearance, height, accent, education, thinking style, voice or social class).

Taking a systemic view

In order to move out of our current stagnation with Diversity and Inclusion, there is a real need to challenge and shift the paradigm: to detach ourselves from the linear business case model, the obsession with metrics alone and the traditional role of HR.

We need to take a wider, systemic approach

If we continue to focus solely on the business case and the statistical link between diversity and profit, we end up making only small changes to process and policy (the ones we can 'prove' improve the bottom line in the short term), without any larger cultural shift. This is why we have not seen much sustainable progress in Diversity and Inclusion thus far.

The approach in this book is based on mindset and culture change. It rests on principles of Organizational Development, and addresses the problems we have identified above. The approach is:

- *Holistic*: It is not narrow; it takes a systemic view of the organization, the person within the organization and the organization within society and the world.
- *Congruent*: It aligns itself with organizational strategy, purpose, values and operational context.
- *Iterative*: It is a systematic and strategically sequenced approach, where interventions are not thrown together randomly but where the order is intentional and thought-out.
- *Imagination*: It starts with a radical re-imagining of what is possible; it challenges norms and inspires people to think and act differently. It is a fundamental re-wiring of how we think about ourselves, and each other, and how we make decisions.

---

[1] The Bottom Line: Corporate performance and women's representation on Boards (2004–2008), http://www.catalyst.org/knowledge/bottom-line-corporate-performance-and-womens-representation-boards-20042008, Retrieved 23 September 2014.

[2] Women Matter: Gender diversity, a corporate performance driver, http://www.europeanpwn.net/files/
mckinsey_2007_gender_matters.pdf, Retrieved 23 September 2014.

[3] Why Corporate Boards are so White and Male, in One Chart, http://www.businessweek.com/arti-
cles/2014-09-12/why-corporate-boards-are-so-white-and-male-in-one-chart, Retrieved 23 September
2014.

[4] Castilla, E. J., & Benard, S. (2010). The paradox of meritocracy in organizations. *Administrative Science
Quarterly*, 55(4), 543-676.

Chapter 3

The case for change

Chapter Outline

Why is Diversity important now?

Human beings have always struggled with difference and tackled it through words, policies and political actions, often with swords, knives or bullets. Today, around the world we see many examples of failed attempts to deal with difference as cultures or ideologies clash. When we cannot see eye to eye, we tackle our differences through war and force.

While working on this book, we spent some time in Krakow, Poland, and we visited the Nazi death camps of Auschwitz and Birkenau. We had previously visited 'The Killing Fields' in Cambodia, and like many others, we remain disturbed and confused by genocide in human history. Krakow and Phnom Penh have witnessed untold horrors that humans inflicted on each other. Ancestors of those who live here now have seen a history of wars and pogroms that took place in the same physical space. We learnt that the decision to create the death (labour) camps near Krakow was due to the central position of the town. It served as a mid-point for the railways across Europe – a very practical choice. These are places where people from different groups have met, traded, crossed paths and sometimes, as cultures and ideologies clashed, killed each other. It is not a stretch to speculate that such a powerful history gets incorporated into the fabric of a culture, and that intangible sense of fear or unease is passed down with generations sharing the same space.

Violence of this kind arises from the self-interest of some who feel they are protecting themselves or a group they belong to, or perhaps it is for profit at the expense of others or a deep-seated bias against another group or a warped sense of duty. The citizens of nearby towns such as Krakow claimed ignorance of the horror in their neighbourhoods, or perhaps they were powerless to act in defence of their neighbours in the face of military oppression. What would happen today in such a scenario? Have we changed and evolved since those horrors? Would we respond differently to injustice at this scale today, and are we equipped to avert such horrors in the first place?

Our differences and similarities (e.g. on matters of national interests, skin colour, religion) have always been the root of trade agreements, politics and war. In our globalized world, we have to learn new ways to work and operate together – and how well we can do this comes down to how we deal with our differences. Bias against others, and inequality, blocks us from working together effectively and achieving our collective potential.

A small percentage of the world's population holds the majority of the wealth, health and quality of life. People die of hunger every day and many lack access to clean water and sanitation. It is not that we don't have enough resources. The problem lies in how well we are able to distribute them and take care of each other. Dr Anita Nowak[2] says this hinges on empathy. Do we see our fellow human beings as 'we' or 'them'? And what makes the difference?

A globalized and networked world

Workforces are more diverse today than ever before. Yet, organizations are showing achingly slow rates of increase in diversity at the top. Compared to the exponential rates of progress in areas of science, technology and commercial success in the last fifty years, the movement on the diversity front is sluggish.

Globalization and social media have made the issue of difference and diversity more acute. The world is getting smaller, news and information travels faster than ever before and we are constantly connected with each other. Today, we are much more visible and transparent to each other in our wealth, poverty and other aspects of difference. Ideas spread rapidly. We hold media devices literally in our hands and are often connected permanently to constantly updated information. We hear what is happening in the world around us in 'real time'. We find out about incidents and reactions as soon as they occur, in 'raw' format, without much time for editing or deliberation. Streams of information fed to us through the media constantly shape our ideas and opinions. This creates urgency and opportunity. We can leverage this potential for globalized media to create unity or allow it to invade our minds with reinforcement of difference politics, leading to conflict and destruction.

Chaos and lack of predictability

Edward Lorenz introduced the concept of the 'butterfly effect': the idea is that a butterfly could flap its wings on one side of the world and set molecules of air in motion, which could then move other molecules of air, causing a cumulative effect that has the potential to create a hurricane somewhere else in the world. So, any miniscule change in initial conditions can drastically affect the final outcome in a dynamic system, making prediction and forecasting almost impossible.[1]

In business, companies now play a role in a complex chain of relationships, servicing and supplying each other, and they are part of a dynamic system that has the same vulnerability to chaos and unpredictability that the butterfly effect refers to. When in 2011 an earthquake caused a Tsunami that hit the coast of Japan, the impact of stopping production in Japanese factories caused a production delay in US factories due to parts not being shipped and slowed delivery of goods and services all over the world. The banks and investors reacted to this, stock prices moved and thus demonstrated how a physical event in one part of the world had impact in other parts as well.

'VUCA' is an acronym developed by the military to describe how increasingly unplanned events are the norm, and that organizations need to be ready to face the unpredictable. V stands for volatility (the speed and nature of change today), U stands for uncertainty (low level of predictability), C stands for complexity (multiple factors and forces that confound the situation) and A stands for ambiguity (mixed meanings and lack of clarity). Together, these represent the current and future context for organizations, and challenge an organization's (and leaders') ability to plan, prepare and forecast.

In order to survive in a VUCA world, it is imperative that organizations are agile and innovative, by fostering creativity, connectivity and collective wisdom. Often, what blocks the organization from innovation is bias and lack of openness at the individual, team or corporate level. Inability to work with difference leads to stagnation. This is where the work of diversity and inclusion becomes critical to business success. It is not about a superficial or statistical link between 'diversity' and 'profit'. It is about noticing the obvious: that as the world becomes more connected, interdependent and unpredictable, we will have to rely on our relationships and ability to work across difference in order to continue to survive, innovate and create.

This brings a new requirement for organizations to consider themselves as social/global citizens. They are part of the cultural ecosystem. They are potentially affected by everything and they have the potential to impact everything that goes on in society around them.

Role of organizations in society

Large organizations are a microcosm of the globalized world we live in, and hold significant power in shaping our lives, ideas and our cultures. Many multinationals are now larger than some countries in terms of size (number of employees) and economic influence. Large corporations have the power to affect politics, not only through financial influence and lobbying, but also through their infrastructure and their ability to transfer resources; they co-operate across borders to enforce policies that affect people globally. This can take the place of governments who may be restrained by national politics or too caught up in national self-interest to have the same effectiveness at an international level.

Global corporations operate, legally, with similar rights to individual citizens and enjoy a level of 'quasi-citizenship'. They impact society as never before, influencing the environment, consumer choice, politics and civil liberties. Large multinational organizations, government departments and public service boards all play a part in influencing society. Global corporations have the power to shift public opinion, to influence the media and to manage the resources and products of the planet upon which our civilization depends.

Should a sector of society this powerful not be accountable to set or at least uphold certain values for wider society? Can organizations be held accountable in the same way as individuals for doing right and wrong? Is there an ethical responsibility, a purpose, alongside the profit-driven business case, for organizations to consider tackling bias and prejudice within society?

The modern corporation, by its inherent purpose, serves society. Pharmaceuticals, food and financial services, for example, are not just businesses. They provide crucial services and products that sustain the population. Media doesn't just report news, it shapes public opinion. These organizations have an innate responsibility to do their work in an ethical, equal and efficient way.

Organizations are at the front line of how different parts of the world interact as commerce becomes more global. Many companies now operate across national borders. This is a significant opportunity to build an inclusive approach that has a positive effect on the different communities and countries served. This goal does not preclude the pursuit of profit. It sits alongside commercial goals and implies becoming more competitive in an increasingly globalized context.

An example from a leading FMCG company[3]

The company was looking at gender diversity in Saudi Arabia, where they saw an opportunity to bring more women into the workforce. There were many cultural challenges as women are separated from men publicly and don't really work side by side here. Still, the company persevered because they saw gender diversity as a key competitive advantage (especially considering their largely female customer base). Initially they just hired female contractors and kept them at a separate site. In 2004, they became the first fast-moving consumer goods company in the Kingdom to be granted a licence to employ women. Since then, they have hired full-time females, they train staff on diversity and inclusion and they have developed programmes to retain and mentor women. To comply with local culture and laws, they established a policy that enables a male relative to accompany a female employee travelling for business.

Today, 15 per cent of their Saudi workforce is women, across a wide range of commercial disciplines (Finance, HR, Sales, Marketing, etc.), with the same benefits and career opportunities as men.

Through careful consideration of local and organizational culture and building practices that are aligned and intentional, they have managed to make a difference not only in changing their workforce demographics and increasing their competitiveness, but also in impacting local culture and creating opportunities for women socially.

Organizations can potentially be beacons of how the world can effectively deal with difference. They can become places where inclusion and empathy are fostered, and through doing so, they can influence change in the wider community.

Consider the impact that a positively empathic and inclusive organization could bring to realizing the potential of employees globally, and the impact on every supplier and customer – and in turn, the impact that their employees, suppliers and customers could bring to their communities, families and nations.

Today, globalization, the internet, social networks and international trade and travel present connections on a scale never experienced before. These major changes in global human experience make diversity and difference a critical aspect of ensuring relevance, success and competitive advantage today – for us as global citizens and also for our corporations that seek to be part of a global economy.

Opportunity for renaissance and the Golden Rule

There is an opportunity for a renaissance now: in how we consider the workplace and society and the link between the two.

Through history there has always existed a maxim across most religions and civilizations, called the **Golden Rule**, which acts as a guiding principle: *One should treat others as one would like others to treat oneself.*

This refers to engaging in a 'reciprocal', or 'two-way', relationship between oneself and others. This implies having empathy with others and perceiving others as the same as oneself (and deserving of the same respect and treatment).

Corporations need to be able to ask and then provide satisfactory answers to the question, 'How does the business that we are in contribute to the common good?'

Creating an inclusive environment is part of the ethical duty of corporations. Being open to different perspectives enables organizations to create workplaces where individuals are valued regardless of background and where the collective decisions of the organization do not do harm to any groups due to prejudice or ignorance. A focus exclusively on profit, without due attention to creating an intentionally ethical and inclusive culture, can replicate and exacerbate the inequalities in society and history.

Punishment of corporations and attempts to change society through legislation alone will only drive compliance rather than genuine change. It is important to *feel a sense of societal duty towards inclusion intrinsically.* A further proliferation of rules and fear or punishment will not positively impact the free market–based society or the entrepreneurial spirit that progress demands and which society needs in the long term. Inclusive organizations and societies cannot be created through sanctions, quotas and targets – they will evolve through intentional attention to human behaviour, mindset and culture.

[1] Kellert, S. H. (1993). *In the Wake of Chaos: Unpredictable Order in Dynamical Systems.* University of Chicago Press, Chicago.

[2] https://www.youtube.com/watch?v=BoEC7qMvTFE, Retrieved 1 April 2015.

[3] P&G Diversity and Inclusion Annual Report, http://www.pg.com/en_US/downloads/company/purpose_people/PG_DiversityInclusion_AR_2012.pdf, Retrieved 1 April 2015.

The Causal Map

The six lenses

Chapter Outline

Before understanding the impact of diversity and inclusion at work, we have to understand where ideas of similarity and difference come from and how they affect the way people think and act. In this section, we introduce a 'causal map' which describes a range of social, psychological and organizational theories and factors that influence how we think, feel and relate to each other, how groups operate and how diversity and inclusion plays out at work.

Diversity and inclusion is not just a workplace issue

It is a human issue, derived from thousands of years of evolution in terms of how we think about ourselves, others and the world around us. Looking for patterns – similarities and differences – is a natural and instinctive process: from an early age, we learn by making rules and categories in order to simplify information. Even very young babies form categorical representations of animals, pictures, shapes and faces. That is how we represent and make sense of the world around us. We learn by making associations. Furthermore, putting ourselves into groups and having a need for belonging are rooted in survival. Many wild animals travel in packs because this helps them come together to capture prey or defend themselves and their territory from predators.

Therefore, when we meet or see someone, we immediately notice aspects of their identity, such as skin colour, gender, voice, accent and clothing. We notice these things because we are psychologically wired to look for similarities and identify members of our own 'group' very quickly. We are also psychologically wired to gravitate to those who we see as similar to us, and to favour those we see as members of our own 'in group'. Someone who says they 'don't notice' skin colour or gender when they are talking to someone is either lying or lacking self-awareness.

The problem is not with the noticing, but with the assumptions, biases and errors that go along with categorization. How we interpret or make sense of categories is limited by the experiences we have had. When we come across something new, we try to understand it by making links with something we already know. When we see something similar to (or which fits with) something old (i.e. something we have seen or heard or been told before) we tend to lump the two together in our minds, and we may also make the assumption that they are the same and they work in the same way. This kind of association and categorization is not only naturally evolved, it is also necessary for our survival. We don't have the time or cognitive space to 'start from scratch' in making sense of everything we see – we have to make links and quick judgements. These judgements can be correct and appropriate but they can also be incorrect if our experience is limited. That's when they lead to errors in judgement and to prejudice, bias and discrimination.

So how then do we tackle the issue of diversity and difference?

Many diversity specialists talk about the need to be 'colour-blind'. This does not work. Colour, along with gender and age and all our other characteristics, is an important and relevant part of who we are, a part that we cannot and should not ignore.

We need to examine our thinking at two levels

At an individual level, we all have our unique personal histories and experiences, which create our beliefs, our sense of identity and our values. These beliefs and values then influence how we interpret our experiences and interactions, who we are drawn to, who we trust, what biases we have, how we make decisions and how we behave.

At a group level, when we come together as a group (as an organization or a social group), we start to build a collective history and create group identities and norms. As organizations are formed and grow over time, they develop a certain unique identity and culture. Organizational identity is influenced by the people within it, by the context it operates in and by its experiences.

It's about culture

A recent survey by McKinsey on diversity and gender[1] showed that cultural factors were more crucial in enabling women to reach senior levels in organizations than individual factors. The culture of an organization has a huge influence on how confident women felt about succeeding. This goes some way in explaining why diversity efforts thus far have had limited success. HR departments everywhere have been focusing solely on specific practical measures (e.g. to recruit, retain or develop female staff), rather than looking at the crucial cultural factors that make such a big difference - that is what is it like for women (and men) to work here. The report recommends that we need 'to ensure that corporate culture supports—not hinders—the ability of women to reach top management ... companies must address mind-sets and develop a more inclusive, holistic diversity agenda'.

And of course, it's not just the culture of the organization. After all, organizations don't exist in a vacuum. As discussed in Section 1, they are subject to the influence of the wider cultural and social context. Particularly in large, matrix organizations, national cultures and occupational subcultures become much more relevant where people from different backgrounds are working together in teams or in the same location. Imagine, for example, a setting where a female doctor from India working with a male nurse from Serbia in a large public hospital in East London. This is where the corporate culture of the National Health Service, the occupational cultures of 'doctors' and 'nurses', and the national cultures of India, Serbia and the UK interface. Too often in diversity efforts, one axis of culture is explored without enough attention being paid to the interplay of different types of cultures.

Take a wider view

It has been argued recently that in order to address the complexity of difference today, what is needed is a 'diversity science',[2] which will take into account the various ways in which we *create* and make sense of categories and group differences, as well as what impact this has on us as individuals and as a society. This means recognizing that categories of difference such as race are not absolute and they do not just occur naturally. They are created and reinforced through daily interactions. Individual psychology is affected by culture and society, and individuals, in turn, shape culture and society. Intergroup behaviours should therefore be viewed through a psychological as well as a sociocultural lens. This means taking into account not only of how humans behave, and the impact of bias and prejudice inter-personally, but also the greater cultural and structural context, including institutions such as the law, media and education.

This book attempts to provide one road map for how this can be done in organizations.

First, in this section, we take a step back to look at the bigger picture of where we are. We draw on the social sciences to see what they tell us about human behaviour and culture. We attempt to map the vast array of individual, organizational and social factors that influence how people and groups act and make decisions.

While this is not the output of a systematic, academic review (and it is certainly not an exhaustive list), it is a framework based on some classic and some emerging social-psychological theories, coupled with the authors' observations through decades of practice in the area of personal and organizational change.

We propose six categories or six *lenses* through which to view a situation. These lenses provide different ways of understanding and making sense of what might be happening in a particular relationship, group or organization. They can help identify where certain practices or behaviours come from or where barriers exist, and consequently, what approaches or tools might work best in that context to create a change. The 'causal map' presented in Model 1 outlines these six lenses, which can be used as a diagnostic framework to understand culture.

Model 1: The 'Causal Map': Drivers of culture

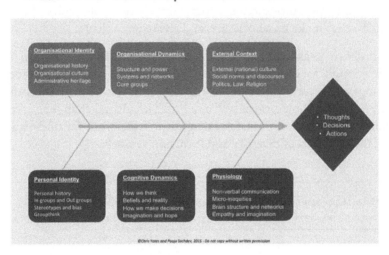

- *Individual or Personal Identity*: how people define themselves, what groups they associate with, how they relate to others
- *Cognitive Dynamics (How our minds work)*: how we think and make judgements, how we develop beliefs about what is normal and good – and how this affects what we see as possible
- *Physiology*: the role of the physical body, non-verbal communication, and how the brain works
- *Organizational Identity*: how the company defines itself, organizational culture, history and the impact of the founders on core beliefs and norms

- *Organizational Dynamics*: how organizational structure and process impact the way things get done, who makes decisions, how decisions get made and how power is distributed
- *External Context*: the wider context within which the organization exists; society, country and national culture

All the above micro and macro factors affect how we as individuals, as managers and as organizations make sense of the world and therefore, how we make and enact decisions at work. We decide who we sit next to, who we hire, who we include, who we listen to, what we aspire to, what we achieve, how we assess and work with others, and how we define, measure and acquire success. Ultimately it is these decisions – big and small – that make us who we are, and create our culture.

In order to create real and sustainable change in an organization, it is not enough to simply make changes to process and policy. Process change, on its own will make little difference in the long run without an individual psychological as well as a broader cultural change to accompany it. This section provides a diagnostic framework for understanding the *precursors* of diversity and inclusion at work.

---

[1] Women Matter: Making the breakthrough, March 2012, mckinsey.com.

[2] Plaut, V. (2010). Diversity science: Why and how difference makes a difference. *Psychological Inquiry*, 21: 77-99.

Personal identity

In this chapter, we look at the first 'lens': personal identity. Personal identity is a sum of all the distinctive ways in which we, as individuals, define ourselves. It includes our gender, age, race, occupation, faith, etc., as well as our relationships and group associations. This concept is key to work on diversity and inclusion because it determines how we perceive ourselves as being similar to or different from others and forms the basis for stereotypes and biases against other groups. Personal identity is also the basis for choosing particular strands of focus for diversity work. In this chapter, we describe what personal identity is, how group association can lead to biases, generalizations and group-think, and what factors are key to creating a community where different groups can coexist and function well together.

On a mid-week cold night in London, in my early teens, I decided to leave my warm house and head across London to a local 'derby' football match against Fulham. I am a QPR fan. My mother thought that I had gone to bed early and had no idea that I was out of the house. I had enough cash to get to the game and cross the city on public transport. I arrived at the ground late, first night-time away game and first time out late in the city on my own. This was the late 1970s. To be black or brown in London at this time was not always safe. The news showed regular marches by the National Front, an ultra–right wing, fascist and very vocal group. Swastikas were often seen on walls and right-wing messages encouraging immigrants like me to 'go home' (I am London born) were commonplace. This was also the era of the height of football violence in the UK.

When I arrived at the ground, the game had started. I got to the gate but did not have enough cash to get in. I turned and walked away, trying to hold the tears back in frustration but not very well. I could hear the game and crowd in the background. The street was empty, it was raining. In front of me appeared five skinheads dressed in full uniform. They saw me and moved towards me. I was expecting the beating of a lifetime and fearing real death.

'What's the matter nigger' they asked. 'I can't get in, not enough dosh', I reply. 'Are you QPR or Fulham?' Instinctively, I answered 'QPR'. To my surprise and complete relief, my new ultra-right-wing friends not only paid for my entrance, but they bought me a hot drink and food, too. I continued to see them at games since that day. I am included to sit with them, and their skinhead friends on future away trips, on trains and then pubs. Eventually and quickly, I become Chris. To them, my association with QPR was more important than my race. In their eyes, and thankfully for me, one aspect of my identity trumped another, and I was accepted as part of their in-group. It could easily have gone the other way and I may not have been alive today.

What is personal identity

Personal identity

Personal identity is the way we describe ourselves to others or the way we represent ourselves in our mental image of ourselves.

It is what you might say when someone who doesn't know you asks 'Who are you?' This may include references to other people (e.g. you might say you are Mrs Smith's son or Sonia's friend), to personal characteristics (e.g. being strong, or loyal or tall) or to what you do (e.g. your occupation). You may mention your gender, your age, your race or groups you belong to. Invariably, your answers would make reference to types or categories or 'groupings' – male/female, young/old/middle-aged, British/

American/Chinese, doctor/lawyer/engineer, employee/manager, friend/colleague/sister – and make some reference to relationships or groups.

Group identity

That part of our identity that is defined by membership of a certain group is referred to as our group identity or social identity.[1] The groups we identify with and feel we are part of are called our 'in-groups' and others are 'out-groups'.

For example, if you are female, women are the 'in-group' and men are the 'out-group'. Social psychologists are very interested in the concept of identity and in-groups, because it is so important in terms of how we interpret and interact with people and things around us. It drives our meaning-making in social encounters and eventually, our behaviour. For example, I see myself as an Indian, and this is an important part of who I am, so I experience positive emotion and pride when India is depicted favourably in the media or wins a sporting match. If I was not Indian, or being Indian was not an important aspect of how I view myself, I might not have experienced elation, and I may not have been dancing on the streets in 2011 when India won the Cricket World Cup!

Multiple identities

Different aspects of our identity may become relevant depending on where we are and who else is around. When we meet others, we subconsciously make connections (we are both female or both cricket fans), or notice points of difference. These observations then influence how we feel and act.

For example, if I am in a meeting at work and I am the only female in the room, my gender identity might become more salient to me at the time. If, however, in that meeting, there was only one other Asian person besides me, I (and others) might become more conscious of my racial identity. It is a natural tendency for humans to look around and seek identification with others, to ask 'where do I belong?' and who am I similar to and who am I different from.

Certain aspects of identity are 'invisible' – such as political beliefs or affiliations to sports teams – and some are difficult to define. I am Indian by birth, British by passport, and currently living in London, so I am as removed as I can be from American politics. Yet, I felt a surge of pride and happiness when Obama won the US elections. It wasn't just the kind of pride that you might have when someone you support or like or believe in wins an election. It was more than that. It was a sense that 'we' had won. I'm not sure that even I can explain who the 'we' is here, but his victory resonated with some aspect of my personal identity.

What categorizations we use for ourselves and give importance to change with the situation we are in. Imagine that the meeting we were talking about earlier was between two internal departments (e.g. HR and Accounts) discussing what went wrong on a particular project. Let's say I was there with two other HR team members, defending ourselves, and the others in the room were all from Accounts, questioning us. In this context, my identity as an 'HR employee' might become more salient and relevant than my racial or my gender identity. We constantly have multiple identities at play, and a complex range of factors affect what aspects of our identities rise to the top and when and how they affect our behaviour. Not all aspects of one's identity are equally important at any given time.

It's also about time and context more generally. For example, I live in London now, and when people ask me where I am from, the answer is that I am 'of Indian origin'. This is quite a significant aspect of my personal identity here because my skin colour is immediately visible, it is not always the same skin colour as the person I am speaking with (in fact, it is usually not, because people around me come from various parts of the world) and because race and racial identity is part of the common rhetoric in the UK. In fact, we are often asked to self-identify with a particular race on forms and paperwork, which reinforces this categorization. On the other hand, this aspect of my identity has no relevance when I am in India. This is because 'race' as an axis of difference is not salient in that context.

Diversity strands

When we speak of diversity in organizations, we are basically talking about understanding the different, significant ways in which our identities converge and diverge. We focus on aspects of identity that are seen to be relevant or potentially problematic: gender, race, age, faith and so on. This is limiting for many reasons.

Firstly, if none of those axes is salient in your personal identity at a given time, then the whole field of diversity might feel irrelevant to you, when really, diversity and inclusion is about everybody and all kinds of individual differences, not just women, black people, etc.

Secondly, we all hold multiple identities that coexist and interact in determining who we are and what we care about. Being a female Muslim from India is different from being a female Muslim from UAE or a male Muslim from India or a male Christian from India or a male Christian from the United States. Even what it means to be a female British Muslim for one woman might be different from another for whom, say, the religious identity doesn't have much prominence. There are so many combinations and perspectives that single-axis categorization to a large extent washes out important, subtle, individual differences between us and creates generalizations that may end up having little relevance to anyone. Isolating one aspect of identity can be helpful to identify specific issues that affect a particular group, but it can also be limiting and artificial.

Thirdly, creating categories for personal identity is not always a straight-forward task. In the national census of the UK, for example, the categories used to classify race or ethnicity have undergone much debate. Do you say 'British-Asian' or 'Asian-British', for instance? Or do you further differentiate Asian into 'Indian', 'Pakistani', 'Bangladeshi', etc., or not? Why doesn't Asian also include Chinese, Taiwanese, etc., as it does in the United States? What if someone has Asian parents but they were born in the UK and they see themselves as completely British? Should the classification be based on place of birth, or skin colour, or parental place of birth, or self-perception? These are the questions that do, and *should* come up when we are dealing with these categories. It is key to remember that although these categories are necessary to provide some kind of instrument for measurement, they are not set in stone and they are not naturally or biologically created. Like national borders, they are developed by us in order to create some kind of system for understanding key aspects of identity.

In multinational companies, a question that often comes up is how to categorize and keep track of ethnicity across employees in different parts of the world. The answer is there is currently no single set of ethnic categories that will apply to all countries. Whereas 'black and white' might be crucial racial categories in the United States, it doesn't have the same meaning or significance in China, for example. In India, religious identity, place of birth, urban vs. rural, caste, class and geography (State) are far more relevant differentiators. When I am in India, I often find myself telling people I am 'Punjabi' but I have never to this date had to tell anyone that I am 'brown'! The way we draw our group definitions and boundaries is constantly shifting as populations and demography change.

Fluid boundaries

Personal identity is not something that is set in stone. It is not predetermined from the time we are born or even from the time we become adults. It is constantly changing and taking shape as we go through life. We continue to have moments when we give up old identities, take on new ones or redefine ourselves in light of new experiences, events and thoughts.

We negotiate our identities and make conscious and subconscious choices about what definitions we adopt, what we give more importance to and what exceptions we allow ourselves.

Sometimes, we might choose not to discard a particular identity but if there is a part of it we don't like, we may negotiate what aspects to adopt and what to exclude for ourselves. For example, I have met some Muslims who say they do define themselves by their religion and it is an important part of who they are. They will pray five times a day, and yet, they allow themselves the odd drink or they may sometimes eat non-halal food. They have defined for themselves what it means to be Muslim in today's world, and adapted the criteria based on their own beliefs about what is important. While more staunch Muslims might argue that such a person is not a 'true Muslim', it is neither hypocritical nor exceptional. In fact, you could argue that it is a mature way to tackle dissonance between conflicting identities and beliefs. We all have the freedom to choose what labels we put on ourselves, and what these labels mean for us. Yet we don't always realize that we have this freedom.

By remaining oblivious to the power of group identity and bias, we limit ourselves personally. We fail to see that we have a choice, and that we have the freedom to define what our categories mean for us. We can become victims of our own classification and feel helplessly bound by criteria set by others.

Having rigid identities and tightly defined and defended in-groups and out-groups is the root of prejudice, discrimination and social conflict.

Stereotypes and bias

Strong group identities can increase our sense of belonging and esteem, but they can also lead to incorrect judgements about our own and other groups. This is because we don't regard all categories in the same way, or in a neutral way. Categories often come with a set of characteristics that we associate with them – for example, ideas about ways in which women are typically different from men, or stereotypes about older people, or lawyers, or football fans.

Try this riddle:

A father and a son were in a car accident. The father dies and the son is critically injured so he is brought to the emergency room. However, when he gets there the surgeon says, 'I can't operate on him, he's my son'.

What does this mean?

(Most people take some time to work out that the surgeon was the child's mother. Our natural assumption is that surgeons are male.)

The issue of course is that very often, stereotypical characteristics may not fit the person we encounter in a particular situation, and they lead us to make incorrect assumptions. We may not be conscious of the stereotypes we hold or assumptions that we make, but they may nevertheless affect how we view that person and behave with them.

When stereotypes are not in our conscious awareness – they are said to be 'implicit attitudes' or beliefs that we are not aware of. We cannot identify a specific source or experience that led us to hold these beliefs. They tend to be deep-seated and hard to change.

The Implicit Association Test (IAT) is a psychological test based on relative associations between images and words. It asks participants to quickly sort or match words, phrases and pictures in order to measure unconscious attitudes about certain groups.

For example, participants may be asked to pair black and white faces with positive or negative adjectives. Where a bias towards white faces exists, participants tend to attribute positive words with white faces more quickly than vice versa.

The test has shown that most people have an automatic preference for white over black faces. The test is now widely used for training and raising self-awareness of managers in organizations and other research to identify the link between beliefs and behaviour.

There are a number of different tests that measure implicit attitudes but the IAT developed by Harvard University is widely used and available for anyone to take.[2]

Implicit attitudes and stereotypes can affect how we instinctively feel about someone we meet, how we judge other people, how we respond to someone, and who we like or dislike.

Think about the subtle ways in which you may feel and therefore act differently – even simply speak in a different tone – with a new member of your team who is a woman, or a man, or a young new graduate, or a doctor, or a woman wearing a full veil.

In-group bias

Psychological studies have shown that we are more drawn to people who are like ourselves,[3] and we experience some anxiety when confronted with people from other groups, particularly groups we don't have much familiarity with.[4]

We treat people who we see as part of our in-groups more favourably than members of what we consider to be out-groups, regardless of rational evaluation.

A British psychologist, Henri Tajfel, studied this phenomenon extensively in the 1970s. He and his colleagues set up a number of experiments where people who were total strangers were randomly split up into groups, and then asked to take part in an exercise (appreciation of a particular style of art). Amazingly, they found that *even though the participants had not met each other until that day* and had only been assigned groups on the basis of the flip of a coin, they still showed a tendency to think their group was better, and they rated members of their own group as more likeable! That is just how powerful groups – even artificially created groups – can be.

We are biased against out-groups in more subtle ways, too. For example, we tend to assume that, when we meet someone from another group (especially a group we have had less contact with before), the characteristics they display are representative of the whole group or, conversely, that a decision made by the group reflect what each member personally feels.

When I first moved from India to a small town in the United States, I was struck by how little people in that town knew about the rest of the world. I often got asked strange questions such as whether we had a refrigerator at home when I was growing up or if there were cows everywhere on the streets. Very few people I met had come across an Indian person before and I was something of a novelty. In a way, it was amusing, and it gave me the opportunity to re-invent myself. But on the other hand, I felt this incredible burden because I knew that everything I said or liked or did would be seen as a representation of all Indian people – whether it was when I ate dinner or what books I read or how fast I spoke.

Then I moved to London, England, where there is a large Indian community and most people had met Indian people. The reactions I got were completely different. I didn't get any strange questions but very often, people I met would say 'Ah, India? My neighbour's step-son is Indian'. Or 'My college roommate was Indian'. And underlying those seemingly neutral remarks was often an assumption that I was in some way like the other one or two Indian people they knew. People made the assumption that my marriage was arranged, and that my parents were conservative. Whereas in mid-western America I was exoticized and treated like a strange creature, in London, I was put into a box straight away.

We tend to make more allowances for individual differences within our own groups than within others' groups. In other words, we see other groups as more homogenous (they are all the same) while we accept that there may be variability within our own group (we are diverse). Even when we meet people who do not fit the stereotype we hold of their group, rather than changing our stereotypes, we often class the person as an exception so that our (inaccurate) beliefs about the group remain intact.

When in-group members do well, we tend to give them credit for it, by saying it is because of something personal like their skill, and we attribute their failures to external factors like bad luck. We don't give out-group members the same benefit – when people from another group succeed, we are more likely to attribute it to good luck and when they fail, we are more likely to attribute it to them not having the right skills or ability.

These are some of the subtle ways in which group identity and ideas about in-group and out-group affect (and distort) our perception and judgement of others. Most of the time, we are oblivious to these errors and we continue to go about thinking that we are making rational and fair decisions.

Modern racism

Over time, overt, explicit racism has declined, partly in response to changing legislation and social trends: people have become more aware of the 'evils' of prejudice, and social norms dictate politically correct outward behaviour. However, the more subtle forms of discrimination such as implicit/unconscious bias remain prevalent. In fact, because of their subtle, 'under the surface' nature (and in the absence of the language provided by overt racism!), they are harder to detect and deal with. Even where people hold egalitarian beliefs and want to be fair, bias affects people's decisions when they are put under pressure or when the situation is ambiguous (e.g. when candidates for a job are 'marginal', that is not clearly strong or weak, credit is more likely to be given to white candidates than black candidates).[5]

Unless we are very attuned with our 'behind the scenes' cognitive processes, we are often unaware of these biases, and cannot control them. This is the stalemate we are currently at in the Diversity & Inclusion space. Most progressive organizations have, by now, learnt about and accepted the existence of 'unconscious biases'. The work on unconscious bias made huge strides in raising corporate awareness of this psychological phenomenon. Many organizations now run unconscious bias testing, and offer 'unconscious bias training'.

Unfortunately, in reality, these training sessions vary in depth and quality and there is little evidence for their impact on individual decision-making and organizational change. We now acknowledge that biases exist (and the tests can help us identify what specific biases we may hold), but we don't know how to treat or reliably get rid of them. Nevertheless, the introduction of the concept of unconscious bias into the corporate world has at least given us a language for understanding our mental process and talking about the impact on decisions.

Decision-making and groupthink

Members of a group often behave in very similar ways to each other as they feel a need for uniformity as a symbol of belonging. When the desire for group conformity becomes very strong, members tend to minimize any possible disagreement and this sometimes leads to what is known as 'groupthink'.[6]

'Groupthink' occurs where members of a group adopt the same or similar attitudes to strengthen the group bond and avoid conflict between members.

Often, individuals in a group stop thinking for themselves; they actively discourage or silence opposite viewpoints and end up making irrational decisions on the basis of a 'herd' mentality. Feelings and behaviour move towards the group norm and these standards become the individual's standards. This effect is stronger with greater group identification.

Groupthink can be very strong where there is a powerful leader at the top who people are hesitant to disagree with. In these situations, significant decisions can be made without enough critical thinking. It is not an uncommon sight to see a powerful executive with a band of 'yes men' around them. This can create a culture where people don't voice what they really think, for fear of being excluded or removed. Or worse, they don't even know what they really think any more, they just blindly go along with things. Many of the destructive organizational decisions in the last several years can be attributed to this phenomenon, perhaps even the financial crisis of 2008. The large international financial services companies employ some of the most intelligent and qualified people in the world – if you have ever applied for a job at one of them, you would know that they are notoriously hard to get into. So where were these highly intelligent, qualified people when sub-prime mortgages were being overvalued, long-term outcomes were being ignored and financial services companies were making commitments without sufficient capital backing? Why weren't enough people able to identify, challenge and change the bad practices before they got out of hand?

We make different decisions in groups. The presence of our 'group' (even a group of complete strangers or a virtual group) can influence how we behave by making us less likely to think for ourselves. We accept things that we might not otherwise accept because the presence of others can reduce our sense of individual responsibility.

Diversity practices often treat aspects of our identity in a static way, for example, counting the number of black/Asian/White/male/female/heterosexual/ etc. employees and don't pay enough attention to how categories create group identities and how group dynamics operate in the workplace.

Living and working together

Groups give us a sense of belonging and safety but they can also be a conduit for biased behaviour and conflict. One of the ways that is often suggested to reduce intergroup conflict and anxiety is to increase contact between different groups. Through increased contact with other groups, the hope is that our beliefs will then be based on real experience and not what we see in the media or what we have heard from others. This isn't as straightforward as it sounds, however. In some instances, contact with other groups can actually increase feelings of 'us-them', particularly if there is the idea that the two groups are competing for resources that are scarce. For example, one study in London[7] showed that living in an ethnically mixed neighbourhood increases the possibilities for different groups to meet and interact but it doesn't necessarily lead to positive and meaningful contact. Several other factors play a role in determining how ethnic diversity affects 'perceived social cohesion' – age and economic deprivation being two important ones.

It is only a particular type and quality of contact that can create a sense of understanding (rather than tension) that ultimately enhances social cohesion. The same applies to organizations. Throwing people from different groups together without creating the right cultural context won't help and can actually make intergroup tensions stronger. 'Diversity', in itself, doesn't always result in positive connections between different groups or increased effectiveness. For this to happen, diversity needs to sit with some key cultural conditions that help different groups to coexist and cooperate rather than compete and have conflict, for example:

- similar opportunities to succeed
- common goals and positive interdependence so groups are motivated to cooperate with each other, not compete
- little or no competition for scarce resources within the group (real or imagined)
- a focus on what people have in common
- strong and positive relationships between individuals within the group

How much of this resonates with your organization or neighbourhood?

Efforts thus far which have been directed at simply increasing 'diversity' have had limited success because they have not placed sufficient emphasis on the contextual factors that influence how different groups coexist and how well they perform together.

Summary

We all have multiple, shifting identities, which develop and change over time, with different aspects becoming salient in different contexts. Group association gives us a sense of belonging but it also sits at the root of bias and discrimination. Our group affiliations affect our unconscious evaluation of those we see as 'others' and this impedes fairness, diversity and inclusion. The intention to be egalitarian doesn't always preclude us from being prejudiced, but we can work at becoming more aware of our implicit attitudes and proactively seek evidence to counter our stereotypes.

Current approaches to diversity focus on singular 'strands' of identity, which can be limiting and artificial and fail to address the complexity of who we are. Diversity alone is not a sufficient aim. We also need to understand how different aspects of identity affect the way we think about ourselves and others, and how group dynamics operate.

Taking a holistic view means moving the focus away from specific axes of difference, such as gender or age, and broadening our understanding of how humans identify themselves on multiple levels. In order to get underneath some of the cultural barriers to change, organizations need to go beyond simply bean-counting and coordinating networking groups, and attempt to understand the different identities and personal histories that are at play in their context, how different subgroups interact, how cultures develop and operate, and how all these factors influence people to think and act. The iterative approach in Section 3 offers a tactical method for creating the right kind of cultural environment where a diverse group of people can work effectively and collaboratively together.

---

[1] Tajfel, H., & Turner, J. C. (1979). An integrative theory of intergroup conflict. *The Social Psychology of Intergroup Relations*, 33, 47.

[2] https://implicit.harvard.edu/implicit/selectatest.html, Retrieved 10 April 2015.

[3] McPherson, M., Smith-Lovin, L., & Cook, J. M. (2001). Birds of a feather: Homophily in social networks. *Annual Review of Sociology*, 27, 415–444.

[4] Stephan, W. G., & Stephan, C. W. (April 1985). Intergroup anxiety. *Journal of Social Issues*, **41**(3): 157–175.

[5] Dovidio, J. F., & Gaertner, S. L. (2000). Aversive racism and selection decisions: 1989 and 1999. *Psychological Science, 11*(4), 315–319.

[6] Janis, I. L. (1972). *Victims of Groupthink: A Psychological Study of Foreign-Policy Decisions and Fiascoes*. Boston: Houghton Mifflin.

[7] Johnston, R., Poulsen, M., & Forrest, J. (2015). Increasing diversity within increasing diversity: The changing ethnic composition of London's neighbourhoods, 2001–2011. *Population, Space and Place, 21*(1), 38–53.

Chapter 6

Cognitive dynamics
(how our minds work)

This chapter covers the second 'lens': how our minds work. It describes how our beliefs can be irrational and yet powerful enough to change reality. It also covers how we make decisions and judgements, and shows how biased decision-making is at the root of inequality and lack of diversity at work. Finally, we look at how we can use the imagination to open new doors and trigger new possibilities in diversity and inclusion.

We are not rational

Although we may see ourselves as rational beings, the human mind is susceptible to a number of biases - errors in perception or judgement. Prefixed ideas about people or groups can lead to incorrect assessments, even in light of contrary evidence. It's a little bit like wishful thinking; we tend to see and hear only what we want to and what suits us, and we ignore the rest. This is one of the reasons that stereotypes are so resilient regardless of evidence. Even when we meet people who don't conform to the stereotypical beliefs we hold, we are prone to label them as an 'exception'.

Confirmation bias

Even when we think we are objectively seeking evidence, studies have found that we are more likely to seek out, favour and remember information that confirms the beliefs we already hold (and we are more likely to forget or fail to notice information that goes against our assumptions).[1]

In a series of studies in the late '70s, psychologists asked college students to conduct a series of interviews with people to try and decide whether they were introvert or extrovert. They were allowed to ask any questions but in each case, they were given a 'hypothesis' to test – for example, 'find out if this person is an introvert' or 'find out if this person is an extrovert'. In each study, they found that the students chose questions according to what they were told to test, and by doing so, they managed to seek out evidence to confirm the hypothesis they were given, regardless of the person's actual personality characteristics.[2] We tend to easily find evidence to confirm the beliefs we already hold and not to notice evidence that contradicts them.

Beliefs create reality

In fact, our beliefs can actually *create* reality. The same researchers found that what the students were told about the people being interviewed affected their behaviour towards them, and consequently, the response they got. So if they believed they were interviewing an introvert, they were more likely to elicit introvert-type behaviour from people.

It is not hard to see how this might happen in social interactions. If you believe you are talking to someone who is outgoing and sociable, you might be more talkative and friendly towards them, and in response, they would be friendly and sociable back, thus confirming your assumption about them. If, on the other hand, you expected (or perhaps you had heard) that someone was distant and unfriendly, you might be cold towards them and thereby elicit the same response. It's not just our outward behaviour that changes. Our beliefs play out as non-verbal communication (how much eye contact we make, how we greet someone, how open our body posture is), and also affect our physiology (e.g. sweating when we feel nervous). These physical manifestations then influence how we feel, how we position ourselves and how others react to us.

Self-fulfilling prophecy

This process works like a 'self-fulfilling prophecy'.[3]

Self-fulfilling prophecy occurs when beliefs, even if incorrect, are so strong that they actually elicit feelings and behaviours that make the belief come true.

This can be extremely powerful. An important study from the '60s showed the impact of self-fulfilling prophecy in a school setting.[4] The researchers gave students a test at the start of the year and told teachers that the test predicted which students had higher IQs and would make faster progress over the year. Teachers were given names of students who were supposedly expected to perform well (in reality these were randomly chosen). At the end of the year, they gave students a second test and they found that the students who had been identified as showing higher potential actually showed a higher increase in scores than the rest! This finding was groundbreaking, because there was no reason for the students on the list to do better than the others except for the fact that the teachers were misled into having higher expectations of them. In fact, teachers also reported that these students were better behaved and gave them higher subjective ratings. The teachers may subconsciously have given more attention or encouragement to the students they felt had greater potential and unwittingly given them higher confidence and thereby, a greater chance to succeed.

Think, then, about what our underlying beliefs about men, women, Chinese people, older people, Christians, CEOs, secretaries, college dropouts and Harvard graduates can do to the experience we (and they) have when we interact with them at work – and how this can affect their chance of success. Our biases about certain groups are not harmless. They can have a real and significant impact on how people experience work and how they do in life.

Stereotype threat

Negative stereotypes about our own groups can also affect our own performance – even if we don't believe in the stereotype. This is what is referred to as 'stereotype threat'.

In a classic study in 1995,[5] white and black college students were asked to sit a test. They randomly split participants into three groups. All groups took the same test but it was described slightly differently:

1. the test was described as being 'diagnostic of intellectual ability',
2. the test was described as 'a laboratory problem-solving task that was non-diagnostic of ability', and
3. the test was again described as non-diagnostic of ability, but participants were asked to view the test as a challenge

The third group performed the best – that is those who were told that the test was not diagnostic of their intelligence but was a challenge. Being in the first group – that is being told that the test was a measure of their intelligence – had a negative impact on performance. However, it didn't affect everyone equally. What is interesting is that the impact was found to be worse for black than white college students. Why was this the case? The researchers explained this as being an effect of a cultural stereotype about black students being less intelligent. By using the term 'intelligence' in the instruction, this stereotypical aspect of their racial identity was brought to the front of their minds, along with an anxiety about confirming the stereotype. (To support this explanation, they carried out a word completion test and did, indeed, find that black students who were told the test was a measure of intelligence had more automatic thoughts related to the negative stereotypes.)

How might this play out in other contexts? What stereotypical ideas about your gender, age, ethnicity or sexual orientation may be playing at the back of your mind when you go on a date, enter that client meeting, stand up to deliver that presentation or ask for that promotion? And what are the subtle aspects of your environment that bring stereotypes to the front of your mind?

Priming
The effect is stronger when people are 'primed' with words related to their group or the stereotype just before the test or task. This can be as simple as a woman being told she is competing with a man (on a stereotypically male task) or an older person reading something negative about their age group just before a physical task.

Priming occurs when exposure to one stimulus (which can be an image or a word or a feeling) impacts the way we react to something else.

For example, if you are feeling hungry or if you happen to see a big billboard ad for McDonald's on the way to work, you are more likely to pick food-related words out of a word search puzzle. This is because subconsciously, your mind is already primed with thoughts about food. When magicians tell us to pick a random number or a word off the top of our heads, they are counting on the fact that the priming cues that they may have placed around us will influence what we pick – even if we think it is a random choice.

You can't fully control your environment or the stimuli that people encounter on their way to work. However, this research does prod us to carefully examine what we see around us in our typical corporate or office environment, our home environment, and on our streets, billboards and buses. What images and words do we come across every day, and what underlying effect might they have on our thoughts (about ourselves and others) and our reactions, expectations and behaviour? What images do you see on the corporate website, on posters in the offices, on company advertising and on employee communications? What images do you see in the buildings, on the screens and in the board room? What themes do you see and what messages do you hear?

Making fast and slow decisions

Thinking fast
Daniel Kahneman is one of the most prominent psychologists to talk about priming and decision-making. In his bestselling book *Thinking Fast and Slow*, he describes two 'systems' of thinking.

System 1 is associated with involuntary, instinctive, gut reactions (fast thinking) and System 2 is associated with concentrated effort and deliberation (slow thinking). We believe ourselves to be rational beings and therefore we might claim to be usually using System 2 to make most decisions – that is thinking carefully, rationally and making deliberate choices. In reality, however, System 1 is what we use the majority of the time.

This is because we have evolved and developed to the extent that we do not need to go through all the logical steps for every decision we make, and neither is it in our interest to do so. It would be highly inefficient to have to list the pros and cons about what step to take when doing mundane tasks (like brushing your teeth) or in an emergency (when we are in danger). Over time, we learn to make associations that help us remember skills and solve problems quicker, thereby reducing our daily cognitive burden. For example, learning to drive: when we first start driving, we use System 2 because we consciously think about every move; however, over time it becomes more automatic and System 1 takes over. System 1 is also what is sometimes referred to as the 'adaptive unconscious'.[6]

Kahneman characterizes System 1 as 'lazy' by which he means that it takes the path of least effort when it comes to mental energy. So, wherever possible, System 1 will take precedence just because it is easier – even with minimal evidence, System 1 thinking leads us to create quick interpretations and 'jump to conclusions'. This is where instinctive reactions and spontaneous judgements come from. It is then the job of System 2 to step in and check the conclusion by going through the evidence and logic more slowly to ensure it is the right conclusion.

Thin-slicing

Malcolm Gladwell makes a similar distinction in his book Blink, where he talks about snap decision-making or 'thin-slicing', which is similar to System 1 thinking.

Thin-slicing is 'the ability of our unconscious to find patterns in situations and behavior based on very narrow slices of experience'.[7]

Gladwell cites several examples where highly sophisticated decisions are made spontaneously, without careful, slow deliberation or consideration of evidence. Many of his examples are about 'snap decisions' made by experts with a history of experience in the area (e.g. doctors about a patient or specialist art historians about a sculpture), and he shows how they are often correct – even 'dazzling'. In fact, he goes as far as saying that in many instances, more information can actually cloud the issue, and that our unconscious actually delivers a more accurate answer than careful, slow deliberation.

Gladwell distinguishes thin-slicing from 'gut instinct'. Thin-slicing is about very quickly evaluating evidence and making a cognitive judgement. The gut instinct is more about feeling and emotional response. Jonathan Haidt, in his book *The Happiness Hypothesis*,[8] offers a great description of the gut instinct. He describes the distinction between mind and body in terms of the elephant and rider. The rider is the conscious, thinking, reasoning mind and the elephant is the 'gut brain'. While the rider holds the reins, it is the elephant that leads the way. In other words, we are actually ruled by our gut: our automatic, instinctive feelings and snap decisions. He found that people are adept at using rational arguments to support their gut reactions. Psychologists refer to this as 'post-hoc rationalization' – that is making excuses! When our gut has subconsciously made a choice or a judgement, our rational mind is adept at finding a way to explain it so that it sounds reasonable. And we can convince others and ourselves that we are acting rationally, not on instinct.

Thin-slicing, System 1 or gut thinking can be highly accurate, especially when the mind has already had a lot of prior exposure to relevant factors and enough practice in making similar types of judgements. And of course it is necessary and very helpful, especially when time is limited. However, it can also be prone to error. In particular, when we lack proper experience or prior deliberate thought, it can lead us to wrong and even dangerous judgements. As Gladwell points out in Blink, this was the case in the shooting of Amadou Diallo, where four NYPD officers shot the innocent twenty-three-year-old several times and killed him, because they mistakenly assumed he was holding a gun. Gladwell and others have pointed out that they may not have jumped to this conclusion if he had been a white man in a middle-class neighbourhood, rather than an immigrant in the Bronx.

Gun or wallet?
Many psychologists have found support for this claim. In a study entitled 'The police officer's dilemma', researchers asked participants to play a basic video game in which they were required to judge as fast as possible whether someone was carrying a weapon[9] and 'shoot' anyone holding a gun. They found that the decision to shoot an armed target

was made more quickly and more accurately if the target was black, and the decision *not to shoot* was made more quickly and more accurately if the target was white.

The influence of stereotypes also plays out in everyday interactions.

I recall one occasion when I went to a popular large home furnishings store to purchase a sofa, accompanied by a male friend. The salesman (who I had made an appointment with on the phone and who knew I was female) invited us to sit down and try out the sofa. We probably sat there for about twenty minutes, I would say he probably looked at me (the buyer) twice – just two little glances. His attention was focused on my colleague. When we finally got up to leave, he shook his hand and said, *to him,* 'Call me as soon as you decide'.

Had he paid more attention to me, he may actually have made a sale that day!

This is a trivial example, but it shows how a personal bias affected a salesperson's unconscious assumption and behaviour towards a potential customer, which caused him to lose a sale. Imagine the cumulative effect, if all or most of the sales staff in a company have this bias. Systematic biases can have a significant impact on real outcomes for organizations. Imagine then if most sales people in most organizations have this bias, and you manage to address this and your sales people do not have this bias. Immediately, you have a competitive advantage.

When we are under pressure or when a situation is too complicated, we often become overwhelmed and our rational decision-making process shuts down. In these situations, we become more likely to default to our stereotypes and biases. We can call these 'cognitive shortcuts'. In organizations, very often, important decisions are taken under complex and high pressured circumstances, which creates the perfect conditions for bias to creep in. This is worse when we are tired, stressed or preoccupied with a task (which is true for most executives, most of the time!). Kahneman describes how people who are 'cognitively busy' tend to 'make selfish choices, use sexist language, and make superficial judgements in social situations'.[10]

Most organizations tend to favour decisiveness in their leaders – someone who can quickly make a choice and take action. Do we need to change our criteria of a strong leader as someone who can be decisive, but also think slowly and be deliberative – and know which type of thinking to use when?

While Kahneman says we need to slow ourselves down and use deliberation to check our instinctive decisions, Gladwell, on the other hand, poses a greater challenge. He says we need to also be able to rely on our snap decision-making as it can be so useful and accurate, so we need to work on changing our environments (culture) and actively managing our experiences, so that we are set up with accurate and relevant 'raw data' to make the right snap decisions. How many snap decisions continue bias in organizations on a daily basis?

Environment, imagination and hope for change

Our personal life experiences, the messages we hear, the images we see, our culture, language and peers, all influence how we view the world, what ideas we form, and how we interpret and make sense of our experiences. Our environment and the images we see day to day can bias us to think in a certain way.

Bias cannot totally be eliminated, but it can be reduced significantly through deliberately focusing on the essential criteria when making judgements (and actively reducing our exposure to information that may be irrelevant, distracting, or bring up stereotypical associations. For example, blind auditions (where musicians play behind a screen, invisible to the judges) have led to a significant increase in the number of female musicians being selected because judges' unconscious preconceptions about gender roles (and associating certain instruments with men or women) don't get in the way of choosing the best talent. As a result, the most talented get chosen, regardless of gender, and ultimately, the overall quality of the performance is higher.

The Civil Service in the UK now reviews the resumes of job applicants 'blind' – that is without a name (to remove gender or racial associations), or date of birth (to remove age-related biases). I don't know of any private sector organization that does this way. In fact, what I have seen more often is, when a resume comes into the office, the manager asks around if anyone knows this person (and presumably, can offer some subjective opinion on them?). Or that person's name is 'Googled' so that a whole array of largely irrelevant information can be brought to the surface and subconsciously included in the decision-making process. Being human, we are prone to overestimating our ability to be objective, and underestimating our vulnerability to being influenced by ideas and images we see around us. And yet we are all vulnerable, even the most intelligent and fair-minded of us.

Do a quick word-association test.

Think of the word 'LEADER'. What *images* immediately come to mind?

Reflect, honestly and non-judgementally, on your own personal associations with the word.

Countless studies and researchers discuss the role of the media in creating and maintaining images of role models. Consciously or unconsciously we pick up cues from movies, ads and billboards to make cognitive decisions about what seems 'right' and 'possible' and 'good'. American Television shows such as *Will and Grace* and *Modern Family* have a positive impact on views about gay people among the general public because they portray a wide range of gay characters in a way that evokes empathy rather than only showing tokens or stereotypes. What we see on television represents real life, but it also changes real life, because it subtly alters our attitudes, unconscious beliefs and stereotypes.

Our brain makes linkages between images and reality. Even our deepest, hidden, unconscious attitudes are vulnerable to this. Studies show that after people are shown images of admired and respected famous black people, they tend to have a reduced anti-black bias on the IAT test for some time after viewing the images.[11]

Journalists and others have commented on the role that the character of President Palmer (in the *Series 24*) may have had in helping the election of President Obama to the White House. The US *Series 24* ran in the years preceding the election as a popular primetime show in which the president was a successful and well-liked African American man. On the US television show 'The Daily Show' (which aired on 4 June 2008), the host commented that Obama will be the first African American candidate for US President 'since the first season of 24'. This comparison shows how our minds make strong, subconscious connections between what we see on TV and reality.[12]

It all starts with the images in our minds. If we cannot even *imagine* a female CEO or head of state, how can it ever happen in reality? The first step to real change is imagining an alternative possibility.

Psychologists are now referring to this as the 'Obama effect'. The election of the first black president of the United States has inspired black people all over the country to have a more positive self-image. Just after his election, there was an improvement in black American students' exam performance,[13] demonstrating the power of having a high profile and positive in-group role model. His election has also led to dramatically lower levels of stereotyping and unconscious bias against black people among others.[14]

The high level of exposure to a positive role model that goes against the stereotype leads to a change in our thinking about the group. It means that now, when 'black' is mentioned, it is far more likely that a positive image leaps to mind, rather than a stereotypical negative image from the last movie or news clip we happened to watch. This exposure to something new and powerful leads to a small 'tweak' in our mindset which has a big impact on our implicit attitudes, our behaviour and our performance, even if we don't realize it.

The imagination is powerful

Given how we are affected by what we see and what we can imagine, the question is: How can we open up our brains to allow us to imagine something new as being possible and plausible? How can we 're-wire' our minds in a way that challenges established schemas, cultural norms and stereotypes, and creates new possibilities?

Intergroup contact/imagined contact

One of the ways we can do this on a personal level is to actively seek out new experiences and encounters which will challenge the stereotypes we hold. We can choose to sit next to someone we wouldn't normally or automatically sit next to, forcing ourselves out of our safe 'in groups'. We can go to the Harvard website and take the IAT test to identify what our personal biases are, what groups we tend to prefer and then actively seek out evidence to challenge the stereotypes we hold and reduce our irrational biases.

Some recent studies have shown the impact of even 'imagined' contact with someone from another group. Amazingly, we can reduce our prejudice towards another group by spending just a few minutes simply *visualizing* having a positive interaction with them.[15]

The implications of this are huge. It demonstrates that it's not just real experience that can shift our thinking patterns, but visualization and mental imagery can do it, too. Just imagining something differently can change how we think about it, and consequently change what's possible for us. And if simply visualizing speaking to a person from a different background has such a strong effect on us, imagine the impact of visualizing *being* that person.

A team at the University of Barcelona asked exactly this question.[16] They put people in a virtual reality situation where they took on the persona of either a dark-skinned, light-skinned or purple-skinned avatar – as you might do in a video game – where they could respond to their environment as if it was real, for example, being able to move around and touch things. They wore a head mounted display and a body-tracking suit that captured their movements in real time, so as they moved their arm up, for example, they would see their virtual body move its arm up at the same time. All participants took the implicit association test a few days before, and again after the stint in virtual reality. What they found was that those people who took on the persona of a dark-skinned person showed a significant reduction in their prejudice towards dark-skinned people following the trial![17] That is simply after three minutes of being 'virtually embodied' in a dark-skinned person's body.

This finding is groundbreaking because it challenges the notion that racial bias is too ingrained to change. If this little mental experience can help our brain make new associations about another group and enhance our empathy towards others, then there is hope that using the power of imagination, we can unlock and rewire the way we think about each other.

Summary

We are not as rational as we think we are. We favour evidence that confirms beliefs we already hold, making us blind to the full range of evidence available. This is what makes biases and stereotypes so powerful and resilient. Our beliefs then affect how we act, how we judge others and how others respond to us, creating a self-fulfilling reality. Particularly when a situation is ambiguous or complex, or if we are under pressure to make a quick decision (which is very often the case in today's corporations), our rational decision-making process shuts down and we default to stereotypical ideas (cognitive 'shortcuts').

Biased decision-making is at the root of inequality and lack of diversity at work. To truly address this, we need to examine how we make decisions and what type of thinking we use in our organizations. Decisiveness is a valued trait in leaders, but slowing down and taking time to deliberate over evidence may lead to better decisions. We also need to examine our environment and actively manage what we are personally exposed to: What we see affects what we believe to be real or possible.

In Chapter 15, we give examples of ways in which we can unlock the power of imagination to create new possibilities for organizations through the intentional use of media. In Chapter 16, we describe ways in which we can raise self-awareness and empathy and reduce bias. In Chapter 17, we give examples of tactical measures to reduce the impact of bias on decision-making (e.g. in recruitment).

---

[1]   Nickerson, R. S. (1998). Confirmation bias: A ubiquitous phenomenon in many guises. *Review of General Psychology*, 2(2), 175.

[2]   Snyder, M., & Swann, W. B. (November 1978). Hypothesis-testing processes in social interaction. *Journal of Personality and Social Psychology*, 36(11), 1202–1212.

[3] Merton, R. K. (1948). The self fulfilling prophecy. *Antioch Review 8*(2, Summer), 195.

[4] Rosenthal, R., & Jacobson, L. (1968). *Pygmalion in the Classroom*. New York: Holt, Rinehart & Winston.

[5] Steele, C. M., & Aronson, J. (1995). Stereotype threat and the intellectual test performance of African Americans. *Journal of Personality and Social Psychology, 69*(5): 797–811.

[6] Wilson, T. D. (2002). *Strangers to Ourselves: Discovering the Adaptive Unconscious*. Chicago: Harvard University Press.

[7] Gladwell, M. (2005). *Blink: The Power of Thinking Without Thinking*. Back Bay Books. New York, NY., p. 24.

[8] Haidt, J. (2006). *The Happiness Hypothesis: Finding Modern Truth in Ancient Wisdom*. Basic Books. New York, NY.

[9] Correll, J., Park, B., Judd, C. M., & Wittenbrink, B. (2002). The police officer's dilemma: Using ethnicity to disambiguate potentially threatening individuals. *Journal of Personality and Social Psychology, 83*(6), 1314.

[10] Kahneman, D. (2011). *Thinking, Fast and Slow*. Penguin Books. London., p. 41.

[11] Dasgupta, N., & Greenwald, A. G. (2001). On the malleability of automatic attitudes: combating automatic prejudice with images of admired and disliked individuals. *Journal of Personality and Social Psychology, 81*(5), 800.

[12] https://en.wikipedia.org/wiki/David_Palmer_(24_character), Retrieved 24 Aug 2015.

[13] Marx, D. M., Ko, S. J., & Friedman, R. A. (2009). The "Obama effect": How a salient role model reduces race-based performance differences. *Journal of Experimental Social Psychology, 45*(4), 953–956.

[14] Plant, E. A., Devine, P. G., Cox, W. T., Columb, C., Miller, S. L., Goplen, J., & Peruche, B. M. (2009). The Obama effect: Decreasing implicit prejudice and stereotyping. *Journal of Experimental Social Psychology, 45*(4), 961–964.

[15] Turner, R. N., & Crisp, R. J. (2010). Imagining intergroup contact reduces implicit prejudice. *British Journal of Social Psychology, 49*(1), 129–142.

[16] *Can virtual reality be used to tackle racism?* – http://www.bbc.co.uk/go/em/fr/-/news/science-environment-23709836, Retrieved 21 September 2014.

[17] Peck, T. C., Seinfeld, S., Aglioti, S. M., & Slater, M. (2013). Putting yourself in the skin of a black avatar reduces implicit racial bias. *Consciousness and Cognition, 22*(3), 779–787.

Chapter 7

Physiology (the body and the brain)

Chapter Outline

In this chapter, we look at a few ways in which our physiology (body and brain) plays a role in how we act towards others, in the context of Diversity & Inclusion. We highlight the role of non-verbal communication in everyday interactions, the impact of brain evolution in our response to perceived threat from others, and the possibility for enhancing empathy and imagination by allowing certain brain networks to flourish.

Non-verbal expression and micro-inequities

We communicate with other people all the time non-verbally – through facial expressions (smiling, frowning, laughing, crying), reaching out (shaking hands, embracing or touching), or through subtle body language (e.g. crossing arms, making or avoiding eye contact, leaning forward, sitting up straight or slouching). There is a vast amount of research carried out on how facial expressions and body language communicate basic emotions (such as anger, sadness, joy, fear or distrust). People tend to smile, nod and move closer when they like something or someone.

Non-verbal cues like eye contact, strength of a handshake or tone of voice can give someone a 'message' that they are being listened to, accepted, liked, disliked, ignored or treated with suspicion. Most of us have had the experience of 'hitting it off' with someone where we instantly know that they like us and they approve of us – whether it is a first date or a job interview – we know we are 'in'. This is because we pick up on the cues they give us through facial expressions and open postures.

When we think about how we relate to other people at work or otherwise, it can be a useful exercise to try and monitor our non-verbal and bodily responses. Subtle differences in our non-verbal communication are often more powerful than the actual words we use. At a systemic level, this can create what is referred to as 'micro-inequities'.

Micro-inequities occur when we systematically respond to certain groups of people more negatively at the subtle, non-verbal level.

This happens when, say, without realizing it, you tend to make less eye contact with certain types of people (e.g. someone who is much shorter than you or a woman wearing a veil) or you smile more at certain types of people (e.g. people of the same gender or single rather than married people). This is a natural tendency that plays out socially when we meet people, but it also happens in job interviews and at work, where it can create a different experience for different groups that you come into contact with. At work, we come into contact with social groups whom we may not mix with socially. When organizations look at behaviours they want to encourage or discourage, they tend only to look at the macro-behaviours and what is overtly said, and the micro-behaviours that include subtle body language communication are often missed out, even though discrepancies in these can lead to significant discrepancies in how 'accepted' different people feel at work.

The primal reptilian brain

There is another aspect of our physicality, and that is the brain. Looking at how our brain is structured gives another perspective on where our gut reactions come from.

The most primitive part of our brain (which we share with reptiles) is the brain stem, and this is responsible for survival. It is responsible for basic bodily functions such as maintaining blood pressure and digesting food, but also for the fight-or-flight response when we are under pressure. The limbic system or mammalian brain is responsible for emotions – from basic feelings of fear, hunger and desire, to more complex drives such as love, empathy and imagination. The neocortex, which is the 'thinking' part of the brain, is responsible for higher cognitive functions such as language, logic and conscious thought.

The pre-frontal cortex is a critical part of the human brain because it is the last to evolve and it is responsible for complex conscious processes such as planning, abstract reasoning, decision-making, and problem solving. This is the part of the brain that is engaged when we are trying to decide on and work towards personal goals, understand other people or moderate our social behaviour. This is the part of the brain that differentiates us from other animals, gives us a unique 'consciousness' and makes us who we are.

Yet, this is also the part of the brain that tires easily and shuts down when we are under pressure or feel threatened, allowing the limbic system (the more primitive part) to take over.

When we feel threatened (even if it's an imagined threat to our personal identity or group), we suspend rational thought and empathic reasoning, and our reactions are driven by a (misplaced) survival instinct originating in the limbic system. We tend to generalize more, and we become more prejudiced and defensive.

Rewiring the brain

Developments in neuroscience and the recent burst in research using fMRI technology have given us even more insight into how we are naturally 'wired' to think and react. The field of neuroplasticity has shown that the brain structure is not static and that neural pathways in our brain can and do change. Although neuroplasticity generally focuses on the context of brain injury and repair, it indicates that through practice and experience, we can 're-wire' the way our brains work, and potentially make ourselves less biased.

Jeffrey Schwartz is a psychiatrist and researcher in the field of neuroplasticity and obsessive-compulsive disorder (OCD). In his book

You Are Not Your Brain,[1] he talks about ways in which our actions create habits by carving neural pathways in the brain, and he explains how these pathways can be changed – how actual physical change can take place in the brain – through teaching ourselves to think differently and change our habits, for example using mindfulness or cognitive therapeutic techniques. This means that even deeply ingrained ways of thinking, feeling and behaving can be altered fundamentally (and physiologically) by repeated exposure to new stimulus and new associations.

The four steps that Jeffrey Schwartz outlines in his book are based on cognitive therapy and are aimed at individuals who are trying to change their habits, for example, tackling a phobia or OCD or anxiety. These are:

1. *Re-label*: to identify the thought that we find to be unhelpful or irrational, and call it what it is, which is an incorrect brain message
2. *Reframe*: to recognize that the thought is a false brain message, not who you are
3. *Refocus*: to change your behaviour and/or focus on something else
4. *Revalue*: not to take the false messages from your brain at face value, not to take it for granted and not to give it too much importance

By following these four steps (not as simple as it sounds), he says that you can break patterns of thought and patterns of behaviour fundamentally at the 'brain' level. If this is true, and if deeply ingrained, learned habits can be changed, this should also be true of deeply ingrained bias and prejudice. Can we teach ourselves to be mindful of our thoughts about each other and to interrupt or challenge our negative assumptions about other groups? Can prejudice be unlearnt? Recent developments in neuroscience offer organizations new ways in which we can look to shift our deep-seated biases and 'rewire' our brains to be more objective and inclusive.[2]

Transcendence, empathy and imagination

The concept of 'brain networks' is also helpful in understanding where our reactions come from and how we can adapt our ways of thinking to become more empathic and inclusive.

Neuroscientists have discovered a number of neural networks that exist in our brain, of which the following are understood to be the primary four[3]:

- *The Reward Network*: This network of neurons is responsible for perceptions of pleasure and it responds to anything that gives enjoyment, whether it is physical (e.g. food) or psychological (e.g. praise).
- *The Affect Network*: As the name suggests, this networks controls emotions, or rather, the physiological responses (e.g. heart rate and blood pressure) that the brain interprets as feelings. This is where the 'gut instinct' originates.
- *The Control Network*: This network regulates impulses and behaviour. It activates when people think about long-term consequences, and intentionally focus and manage priorities.
- *The Default Network*: This is the network that is activated when people are awake but not intentionally focused on a particular thought, task or goal.

The Default Network is the network that is engaged when the person is not intentionally engaged in 'work', and yet it is crucial for introspection, imagination, creativity and innovation. It is responsible for our ability for *transcendence* – that is being able to detach from the current situation and imagine being in a different place, time or situation. This ability for transcendence is what creates the space for new ideas and breakthrough thinking. It is also what ultimately facilitates empathy – that is being able to think about things from another's perspective.

At an organizational level, having the opportunity for employees to engage their default networks (not just focusing on task) is critical to enable innovation and transformation, and also to enable a culture of empathy, interpersonal understanding and inclusion. Empathy is linked with imagination because both rely on the ability to see things abstractly from another perspective – whether from another person's perspective or from an innovative perspective. This mental ability – to transcend the physical and immediate reality – sits at the heart of creating innovative, inclusive and high-performing cultures.

Much of the work in Diversity & Inclusion to date is driven by threat and fear – fear of legislation, lawsuits, penalties, backlash or the fear of being excluded, of saying something 'politically incorrect', of being called a racist or of not fitting in. When our actions are driven only by primal responses of avoiding threat, they are limited, defensive and not always reliable or rational. Most of the solutions are consequently aimed at penalizing people and reparation of injustice, whether it is through new laws, tougher policies, monitoring or quotas. We need to allow the 'default network' to flourish, and thereby give ourselves the space to think, feel, understand, create and innovate.

What we need now for bigger and more sustainable positive change is to focus not just on penalties and policies but on how we can create a culture of sharing and feedback – a culture where creative thinking, innovation and understanding are fostered, not just task and output. A culture where we can collectively imagine a better future for us all and we can work collectively towards it, where we are driven not by threat but by our aspirations.

The first and biggest task is to create an ideal, desired end-state that everyone can visualize, aspire to and work towards collectively. We need to use positive motivation and not fear. Feeling threatened and fearful only evokes the narrow, primitive responses of fight or flight, which is counter to the goal of creating more understanding, abstract thinking and empathy.

Summary

When we look at behaviour at work, we need to take into account the subtle, non-verbal aspects as well as the overt and verbal aspects of how we respond to each other and we need to consider the impact of how our brains function.

Our ability to make rational decisions is reduced when we are under stress or feel threatened because we resort to using the primitive, reptilian brain and our reactions can become even more prejudiced and defensive than normal. Actions driven only by fear or threat are limited and defensive.

At an organizational level, creating space for task-free reflection and building a collective aspiration can help to foster a culture of innovation, empathy, imagination and creation. We should ask: Are we, in our organization and in our diversity efforts, driven by fear of penalties, or by a positive collective aspiration? In Chapter 14, we propose a list of questions to consider when diagnosing an organization, including where the impetus for change comes from. In Chapter 15, we outline a method for developing and articulating a collective aspiration through the process of Appreciative Inquiry. This is a positive and effective way to kick-start the process of creating an inclusive and innovative culture.

Principles from cognitive behavioural therapy can be applied at a personal level, to help rewire the way we think about ourselves and others, and thereby shift our biases. We can practice being mindful of our thoughts and judgements, and challenge them rationally as we interact with others. This ability is crucial to be able to counter the impact of bias. In Chapter 16, we list some leadership traits and behaviours that help to foster this capability, for example self-awareness, critical thinking and empathy. We also discuss practical ways in which we can change our ways of thinking, for example by seeking out new experiences and perspectives.

---

[1] Schwartz, J., & Gladding, R. (2011). *You Are Not Your Brain: The 4-Step Solution for Changing Bad Habits, Ending Unhealthy Thinking, and Taking Control of Your Life*. Penguin.

[2] See, for example, work by the Neuroleadership Institute, http://www.neuroleadership.com/portfolio-items/breaking-bias/

[3] Waytz, A., & Mason, M. (2013). Your brain at work. *Harvard Business Review*, July–August 2013, 102–111.

Organizational identity

In the next three 'lenses', we zoom out of the individual and start to focus on the wider group: the organization and society. Like people, organizations also have identities and particular dynamics of how they work.

In this chapter, we look at Organizational Identity. By this, we mean how an organization defines itself and how organizational cultures are formed and evolve. We look at a few different ways to understand culture and highlight the link with structure and power. We emphasize the importance of considering culture in any work on Diversity & Inclusion.

What is organizational culture

Who we are

If you go to any corporate website, you will almost always see a 'Who we are' section. Click into a few of these and it becomes apparent that just like people have identities, so do organizations. Sometimes, the 'Who we are' section will tell you the names (and maybe show you photos) of people on the board. Other times, it will talk about the history of the company, where and when it was founded, by whom it was founded, what it's purpose is, what it believes in, where it operates and how it does its work. All these aspects make a company 'who it is'.

Think, for example, about two large multinational organizations, both selling the same or similar product or doing similar work, such as two large grocery chains, or two large fashion brands. How are these two organizations similar and how are they different? What 'feeling' do they each inspire? Despite doing the same work, what intangible elements make the two companies different? Many things might influence this intangible sense of organizational identity and culture: where geographically it is based, how old the company is, who is the leader, what image they put out publicly, how they have been portrayed in the news and in advertisements, what policies they have and how things are done within it. That's culture.

We have spoken to hundreds of people in organizations about the subject of Diversity & Inclusion, and in the vast majority of conversations, after discussing the merits of one intervention over another, when we finally ask 'What will really make a difference?', we almost always hear something along these lines:

> *I'm not sure a women's development programme or setting quotas is really going to fix the problem. It will help the numbers a bit. You may get another few women making it into management, but it's going to be a struggle in our culture.*

This was the key impetus for this book: If most of us are aware of the fact that Diversity & Inclusion is ultimately about culture, why aren't Diversity and Inclusion efforts being directed more towards addressing culture?

So, what exactly is culture?

'Culture' is what characterizes a group of people. It is the sum total of the ideas, customs, traditions, history, rules and assumptions that are shared by members of a group, that serve as a guide for behaviour. It includes not only visible elements (e.g. dress, rituals, language, food, customs, religion) but also those shared assumptions that exist 'under the surface' and cannot always be seen. This includes basic values, beliefs, unwritten rules about how people interact with one another, and ideas of what is considered normal and right.

The same holds true for organizational culture. Organizational culture refers to those aspects of an organization that make it 'who it is'. It is a particular combination of characteristics that derive from who founded the organization, where it was founded, what its original aims were and what the operating context has been. Just like with individuals, the origin, history and experiences of the organization feed into how it now defines itself and operates. Culture includes the visible and invisible elements that make it a particular 'kind of company' in terms of what it is like to work there and how it operates.

Where does culture come from?

The company's assumptions and guiding principles often come from the personal philosophies and habits of the people who founded it. This is sometimes referred to as the administrative heritage[1] and it impacts an organization's propensity and capacity for change. The basic purpose, values and principles upon which it was founded become part of the fabric of an organization – its deeply embedded cultural foundation.

A strong hierarchy (where the culture might be described as highly driven by roles and rules) presumes a particular view of human beings reminiscent of McGregor's famous theory X[2] – that is, that people are basically lazy and will avoid work unless closely supervised and motivated by self-interest. If the founders of the company had held a different basic belief about human nature (e.g., Theory Y, that human beings are self-motivated, ambitious, want to do well and can find work fulfilling under the right circumstances), they might have set up the organization differently. They might perhaps naturally be inclined to relinquish some control and operate more as a clan or adhocracy, giving employees more leeway to make decisions and be creative.

These basic ideas about what is right, good and ideal originate in the founders and the history of the organization, as well as in societal norms. They pervade organizations and form the driving principles for actions that shape the culture. Over time the culture naturally evolves as the organization lives through different experiences and external environmental changes, and how it changes depends on how it deals with problems it faces. If not addressed intentionally, culture normally evolves in a responsive way.

Three levels of culture

One of the most notable writers on the subject, Edgar Schein, describes organizational culture as having three levels[3]:

1. *Artefacts and Behaviour*: these include visible structures (e.g. buildings, rooms, décor, layout, furniture) and the physical surroundings as well as expressed and typical behaviours (e.g. office humour, dress codes, urban myths and stories that are distinctly recognizable as being part of the culture of the organization).
2. *Espoused Values*: this is what the organization says they believe in, how they represent themselves publicly and in official statements (e.g. stated values and mission statements, corporate policy documents, advertising, marketing and internal 'mantras' that employees are asked to live by).
3. *Basic Underlying Assumptions*: these are the 'real' values; they represent the core beliefs of the organization. They are the unwritten, unspoken, taken-for-granted assumptions and rules by which the organization is run. Sometimes these are so ingrained in organizational mindset that it is hard to even identify them explicitly, though they are the real driving force for how decisions are made, what is valued and how the organization defines success.

In most organizations, there is invariably a clash between the behaviour, values and assumptions, and this is where problems arise. When you look closely at any organization, you often find that the stated (espoused) values do not always correspond with how the organization actually acts and there may be a disconnect somewhere.

It is important to pay attention to congruence between stated values, outward behaviours and underlying assumptions in organizations. It is also important to consider how well all these three aspects of culture are aligned with:

- what stakeholders want
- what employees want
- what customers want
- what shareholders want and
- what society wants

In many organizations, the reality is at odds with the aspiration.

One company I worked for some time ago described itself as being a meritocratic, non-hierarchical company that valued knowledge and expertise over status and title. And yet, when you looked around you at the way the office was structured (at least the London office), senior-most managers had their own private offices (with the doors being closed most of the time!) and allocation of parking spaces was based on role level and tenure. I still remember getting my first hard-earned promotion at that firm, and (despite no noticeable change to my pay check) how pleased I was to be moved to a window seat! The way the desks and furniture is placed in an office may seem trivial but it can have significant meaning, and it can impact how people interact with each other, how they feel on a daily basis, what is valued and what sort of working culture is created.

Sometimes the processes may be set up in a way that inadvertently motivates people to act in ways that are counter to the stated values. One company recently experienced a spurt of expansion in a number of new countries and sectors. Following this growth, the board recognized that in order to function well across the globe, employees of the company needed to work together with their new and old colleagues in different areas. And so, a great deal of emphasis was put on having a spirit of 'cooperation not competition' and this included 'cross-team collaboration'. Different areas of the business were asked to work together, and the vision was that ideas, knowledge and resources would flow smoothly across geography and division. In practice, however, each department's bonuses were based on their individual productivity. Productivity was measured by sales and client contact. Whoever claimed a sale or ended up as the main client contact, was awarded the end-of-year bonus related to that project. In this context, while team managers may have wanted to cooperate with each other (and in most cases, they would ultimately benefit from doing so), they were often afraid that giving away any information on clients or new leads would mean that they might lose part of their bonuses to another team. So they ended up consciously or subconsciously 'hoarding' information, and being reluctant to help each other. As a result, teams did not know what was going on in other parts of the business, clients became frustrated with their disconnected experience with the organization, and the company got a bad reputation for inconsistent and disjointed customer service. This was especially embarrassing for a firm that had publicly touted collabo-ration and cooperation as one of its key values, and was trying to build an image of a strong, global brand. What happened here was that behaviours (i.e. practices, policies and reward structures) were not aligned with the stated values.

On a deeper level, there are times when the stated values don't corre-spond with behaviour, not because of bad process or practice but because the values do not reflect the genuine underlying assumptions that the organization holds. In other words, an organization says one thing but deep down, it actually believes another.

For example, one large British organization has been grappling with the issue of flexible working recently. Consultants had advised the board that giving employees the option to work in a flexible environment was better for business because it would help to attract 'Gen Y' employees[4] and retain working parents and so it would be good for diversity. It would also give the organization a better image as a modern, twenty-first-century employer, and all the competitors were doing it. So money was spent on bringing in new technology and re-designing offices to allow people to use laptops and 'hot desk', to log in and work from home, and to dial in to 'virtual meetings'. In record time, the environ-ment had changed and there was a buzz in the air about the new way of working. Some people were excited about what opportunities this might bring them in terms of balancing their work with their outside commit-ments – does this mean I can go to the gym in the morning every day and work an extra hour in the evening? Does this mean I can leave at 4 p.m. every day, pick up the kids and log in to finish my work after they are in bed at 8? Does this mean I can work from home during the train strike, or leave early this Friday and work a couple of hours on Saturday? While many employees were filled with curiosity and excitement, others were nervous, in particular some senior managers who had been with the organization for many years and had become used to a particular way of working. Although they attended and nodded in agreement with all the communication about the new ways of working, deep down, they retained the belief that 'work' means being somewhere physically, within regular office hours, and they just could not get their heads around the concept of work being virtual. Because of this, although they had to allow their employees to work flexibly, they did not really believe an employee was working if they were at home, and they did tend to subconsciously favour those who they had more 'face time' with in the office – regardless of the actual output of work. Unfortunately, this mentality wasn't restricted to a few managers but most of the senior managers, and therefore, it became a pervasive, though unspoken, norm. Employees soon learned that while on paper the organization supports flexible working, they may be subtly penalized if they 'take advantage' of the policies too much. There was a disconnect here, between the outwardly stated values and the genuine, underlying beliefs in this organization. While the process and technological changes had been carried out smoothly, what was missing was mindset change, without which the reality lagged behind the aspiration.

Because there is often a disconnect between values, behaviour and underlying assumptions, you can't simply look at what an organization does, or even what its stated values are to determine what the culture is. You need to examine all three levels of culture, you have to take time and critically analyse what you see and hear, question traditions and norms, and reflect deeply on what things are really like and why things are the way they are.

The idea is to go below the surface. Simply looking at what the organization says and even what it wants in principle isn't enough – you have to look at what really happens – the visible and the hidden processes by which things get done.

Examining culture is more complex than it sounds. Not only are aspects of it invisible, but in larger organizations, there may also be variations across different parts, with subcultures in particular departments or locations, depending on what sort of leadership or experiences that area has had. Certain occupations or areas of work sometimes form 'subcultures', which exist within as well as across organizations, for example doctors, call centre workers or travelling sales people. People doing the same type of work may have more in common with each other (and they may have their own unique culture) that can sometimes supersede the culture of the organization (or organizations) in which they work.

In multinational organizations, the organizational culture also interacts with the local, national culture in different parts of the world – and where people move between countries, they have to juggle what they know and believe from their 'culture of origin' with what they may confront in the new cultures in which they live. In the modern-day, large-matrix global organization, how do you go about defining and describing culture, particularly taking account of visible and hidden elements, and also of the multitude of intersecting (corporate and national) cultures that may be at play?

Describing culture

There are many theoretical ways in which organizational culture is described. For example, Charles Handy[5] offers a simple classification. He describes four types of organizational cultures:

- Power culture
- Role culture
- Task culture
- Person culture

The *power culture* may be depicted as the sun (with rays coming out of it) or a spider's web, with the most important and powerful people sitting at the centre, from where control is tightly held. It is typical of small enterprises. Things get done quickly because decisions are made by the people at the centre rather than by committees. This can be very efficient but it relies on the capability of the few in the middle, and there is a risk of the centre losing control if the company expands too much. The closer you are to the middle in such a company, the more power and influence you have. The main focus of employees here is to properly interpret and carry out the mandates from the centre. There are few rules and leaders exercise control by choosing the right people who they can trust to carry out their aims. It can be a competitive and sometimes harsh environment but it is simple and efficient as decisions are made quickly by the few in power.

The *role culture* might be depicted by an image of a building, or a temple, with a roof and supporting columns. A small group of senior managers sits at the top (the roof), and they are supported by specialized functions (the columns). Employees are seen as fulfilling the responsibilities of their particular roles, and all interactions and decisions are carried out on the basis of formal and logical rules and procedures. Power lies in particular roles not with people, that is with whoever holds those roles at a given time.

The *task culture* is characteristic of organizations where work is often carried out by matrix teams or cross-functional project teams or task-forces. The focus is on the task and getting the job done. People from different levels and areas may work together and power doesn't lie in one area or just at the top – it is spread across the organization. Such a culture can be represented as a net, with the power concentrated on the knots, that is where different areas cross over to make things happen. Teamwork and output is valued over and above personal goals and styles, and power lies not in particular positions but in having the right expertise.

The *person culture* is one that is focused on the people within it, and their personal motivations. It is obviously not one that is very common in corporations with commercial goals. It does not have a particular structure, people are loosely connected in ways that suit them and power lies with knowledge. People tend to do what they are good at and are respected for expertise.

In reality, most organizations today are probably a combination of two or more of the above types, and they also change with time and context. An organization that started off being person-based may become task-based as it grows and expands, or an organization that was originally task-based may become more power-based with new leadership or more rules-based when there is pressure from regulatory bodies.

However, despite its simplicity (or perhaps because of it), Handy's classification can be very useful, because it really forces you to think about what the most important, central value is in an organization upon which all processes and decisions are based.

- Which of the four types reflects your organization most of the time?
- Which of these types of environments would you personally prefer to work in, and why?
- What type of person would thrive most in each of these?
- What type of person would not thrive in each of these?
- Which of these four types is ideal for what your organization aims to achieve?

Culture and structure

Hardy's four types also make a clear link with structure, highlighting the fact that the culture of an organization is always connected with how people are organized within it.

- What 'shape' does your organization take? Is it most like a spider's web, a roof-and-column or a net? Or is there another shape that depicts your organization more closely?
- Where is the power located, and how does it flow across the lines?
- Does this shape reflect the reality of how communication takes place, and how decisions are made in the organization?
- Is there a different, informal shape that better reflects the reality of how the organization operates?
- What would be the optimal shape for your organization to really get things done well?

A more recent theory by Cameron & Quinn[6] suggests an alternative classification using some of the same principles. They propose that there are two key aspects on which you can rate any organization. The first is whether the focus of the organization is internal or external. The second is whether the organization exercises a high level of control, or it is flexible and gives employees more discretion to act. Based on where an organization falls on these two key dimensions, you can categorize it into one of four types, as follows:

- Low control and internal focus = Clan (Collaborative)
- Low control and external focus = Adhocracy (Creative)
- High control and internal focus = Hierarchy (Controlling)
- High control and external focus = Market (Competitive)

Where the focus is internal and the control is high, you have what they call a *Hierarchy* culture where there are strict rules and procedures and a clear formal structure – similar to the role culture we talked about earlier. Here, efficiency and consistency are highly valued and leaders are tasked with maintaining control and organization.

Where the focus is internal and the control is low, you have what they refer to as a *Clan*, where the priority is the people and the main values would be individuals' development and participation. The leader's role here would be to act as a mentor, and facilitate effectiveness through team-building and engaging employees. These tend to be friendly places to work where team spirit is important.

Where the focus is external and the control is high, you have a *Market* culture, where the organization is driven by achievement of goals, profit and competitiveness. Here, managers maintain a focus on the customer and productivity and their role is to push employees to work hard to meet targets.

Where managers maintain a focus on the external but have a different vision – one of innovation rather than production – you have an *Adhocracy*. Customer needs are important here, but employees are given more freedom in how they are met. New enterprises and think tanks might fall into this category. Agility and transformation are valued, not just numbers.

Think about your organization. How would you describe it in terms of flexibility and external focus? If you had 100 points to allocate, how will you distribute them between the four types above in deciding what your organization is most like? Is it mostly one of the four types or is it a combination of some types?

Now allocate the points based on where your organization should ideally be.

- Where are the biggest differences?
- Where are the largest gaps?
- What change will that shift make?
- Can you think of one or two simple actions that might make a difference?

The research carried out by Cameron and Quinn also found that where the leaders in an organization have capabilities that are in line with the organizational culture, they will be more successful, and so will their teams. So in other words, whether a leader is 'good' or not depends on how well their traits match the culture in which they operate. For example, in a 'clan' environment, it is important for managers to be nice and friendly, where as in a market or hierarchy environment, they might need to be more focused on task. The best leaders (as per ratings by their colleagues), the research found, are those that can adapt themselves to any of the four cultures and behave in an appropriate way.

There are various other classifications for describing culture available today, and it is outside the remit of this book to describe them all. It is important to bear in mind, however, that any classification system is always going to be a simplification because cultures are necessarily complex and multilayered. Labels such as 'power-based' or 'adhocracy' help us to clarify some of the dominant characteristics in an organization and they give us some insight into the basic values that sit underneath it.

What is a 'good' culture?

Think about and describe what you feel would be a 'good culture' for your organization.

- What would it look like on a day-to-day basis, in terms of how people behave?
- How does this fit in with your diversity and inclusion goals?

Just like there is no ideal style of leadership (it depends on how well the style matches the situation), there is no culture that is ideal in an absolute sense. Many specialists in the area of organizational culture have argued that there is no such thing as a 'good' or 'bad' culture – it's about how well the culture is aligned with the aims. And from a commercial viewpoint, this is absolutely true – different cultural 'habits' will suit different strategies. For example, take a large international financial services company that is operating under normal circumstances. What customers value and what is crucial from a regulatory point of view is accuracy, reliability and stability. When you invest your savings with a financial services company, you would like to count on it to keep your money safe, to invest it wisely, to not take unnecessary risks and to be accountable. Under such circumstances, the sort of culture that might work best is one where consistent procedures are in place and sufficient quality checks are made to ensure that accounts are accurate and money is safe. A relatively high level of control may be needed to make the financial services company operate effectively, to meet the expectations of customers and satisfy regulators. But if the same level of control and bureaucracy is applied in an ad agency or a small consultancy or a design company, it would hinder effective operation because it would not give employees the flexibility they need to be creative and innovative, and serve their clients in the way that is expected of them. It's about alignment. Where there is a disconnect between the culture and the employees, the customers, the internal processes or the external demands, this will hinder smooth and effective operation.

One senior woman in a large UK financial services company spoke of her decision to give up her career to look after her children after twenty years of loyal employment:

My boss has always been very supportive of me, and I owe him a lot in terms of the encouragement he has given me to get to this level. But now that I have had my second child, I know that I need to make a choice. Yes, I've read the HR policy for returning mothers and technically, I could apply to work flexibly or part time, but they would never go for it. They would find some excuse to decline my application. You know how it works. On paper, all the senior managers support all these policies but *deep down, they just don't think that this is a place for women.* Very few of their wives work. Or if they do, they work in some nice, female-friendly occupation. And they have a full time live-in nanny looking after the children and the house. So that's the context these senior leaders are coming from, and that's all they know.

They just don't get why I need to leave at 5 sharp to pick up my son at nursery. Of course, I could explain until I'm blue in the face, and I could stay on and fight to keep my place on the career ladder that I'm on, but honestly, how far will it get me in the end? Another rung up? And then it's going to be even harder because there will be even more people to convince that I belong. It's a losing battle. They just don't care.

Summary

Every organization has a unique culture: a complex set of written and unwritten rules that dictate who has authority, position and power, and how different people and teams communicate and interact. Organizational culture determines the basic values and principles upon which decisions are made.

The bottom line is that if you want to change things, you have to look at culture and mindset first to understand why things are the way they are.

You have to look both at the obvious cultural symbols and stated values, but also under the surface at what the unspoken assumptions and norms are. If the culture is at odds with what employees want, what shareholders want, what customers want, or what the values or goals are of the organization, something will need to change to fix the alignment. No intervention or policy will work if the culture is not congruent with it.

The most effective cultures are often those that are created intentionally, and with purpose. Therefore, in order to address diversity, you have to first examine the cultural context of the organization, to understand where it has come from and where it needs to be. Organizational values, structures and culture need to be aligned with Diversity & Inclusion goals; otherwise any efforts would be working against the tide. Section 3 of this book outlines a practical method for understanding and changing organizational culture in this context.

---

[1] Bartlett, C. A., & Ghoshal, S. (2000). *Transnational Management*, Vol. 4. Boston, MA: McGraw Hill.

[2] McGregor, D. (1960). *The Human Side of Enterprise*. New York: McGrawHill.

[3] Schein, E. H. (2010). *Organizational Culture and Leadership*, Vol. 2. John Wiley & Sons, USA.

[4] Gen Y refers to a cohort of people born in the mid 80s and later.

[5] Handy, C. (1993). *Understanding Organizations*. Penguin, UK.

[6] Cameron, K. and Quinn, R. E. (2005). *Diagnosing and Changing Organizational Culture: Based on the Competing Values Framework* (3rd edn). John Wiley & Sons, USA.

Chapter 9

Organizational dynamics

Chapter Outline

In this section, we take a closer look at the organizational processes: how decisions are made, how information flows, how people relate to each other, and who holds power and authority. *Decisions* are the basic unit of organizational functioning: where to advertise a new product, whether to enter a certain geographical market, who to hire as the new VP of Sales, who to invite to a meeting with a new client, or whether to give a certain employee a score of 3 or 4 on their end-of-year performance report. These decisions – big and small – ultimately impact who is included or excluded, and how diverse an organization is.

Power in organizations
Where does power lie?

Take this simple question and see if you can answer it for your organization.

Who, *ultimately*, has responsibility for decision-making in your organization?

- Only or mainly the senior leaders
- Managers at a certain role level and above

- Specially appointed committees or groups
- Certain specific people (not necessarily the most senior)
- Everyone

Power is linked with structure and culture. Going back to Hardy's classification we looked at in the previous chapter, in a 'power culture', all decisions are made by a small group of people at the centre, so the closer you are to the middle, the more power you have. There are few rules because leaders choose people they trust to carry out their orders. In a 'role culture', power lies in position. Hierarchy is important, and authority is based on role and title. Rules and formal sets of guidelines dictate how things are done. In cultures that are more oriented to 'task', power tends to be more distributed across the organization. People are given authority on the basis of expertise and the focus is on getting the job done.

In reality, most organizations (particularly larger ones) will have a combination of styles, and it may vary between departments or managers or location. Even if the overall philosophy of an organization might be to get focused on tasks and teams, for example, rules may be needed in some aspects of the work, such as legal or quality compliance or to satisfy the criteria of external bodies such as industry regulators.

Types of power

Different types of power may exist within the same organization. Some power can be 'legitimate' in the sense that it is official and explicitly given to certain people or positions (through the use of titles or role levels) to allow them to spend money or manage others. Having the ability to legitimately reward people (e.g. with money, time off, recognition) or to punish them (e.g. public criticism or negative reviews/ratings) is an important source of interpersonal power in organizations. People also gain power through informal means, for example, through personal charisma (being liked), expertise (valuable knowledge or skills) or by acting politically (e.g. exchanging information or favours). Power dynamics drive how people behave with each other and how they get things done.

Impact of personal power

It is important to understand the ways in which power changes people as this helps to explain some of the hurdles faced in diversity work. Having power over others (i.e. being able to control resources that others want), even for a short term, has an impact on us physically, emotionally and cognitively. Power can make us more confident, but it can also reduce our empathy with others.

In one study,[1] people were temporarily given a position of power or power-lessness by being randomly assigned to be a 'superior' or a 'subordinate' role. Even though people were classified randomly, those who were positioned as 'subordinates' performed worse on an abstract task they were given. In fact, researchers showed that just thinking about a time when you were powerful improves your creative and abstract thinking.

One rationale for this is that having power makes you feel more distant from others, so you are able to think more abstractly. The down side of this is that it reduces your feelings of empathy and can make you more self-centred.

Physically taking a high-power position (an open, expansive posture such as standing like wonder woman or leaning back in your chair with your feet on the table) for just one minute increases your level of testos-terone (the dominance hormone), decreases the level of cortisol (the stress hormone), and increases your feeling of power and tolerance for risk-taking.[2] This happens to both men and women, and gives some weight to the notion that women in power are, at least in this hormonal sense, 'more like men'.

Taking the implications of these studies together, it means that (although there are individual variations), generally speaking, gaining power makes any of us more confident, dominating and risk-taking. This can enhance performance in many ways – like a self-fulfilling prophecy – and improve abstract thinking. However, it can also make us self-centred, distanced from others, and less able to have empathy.

Think about the consequences of this in organizations and in society at large. The people with the most power to affect others' lives and make big decisions that impact everyone are also least likely to understand others' needs. They are more likely to be dominating, to take risks and to make lapses in cognitive and emotional judgement. Many have spec-ulated that this power and testosterone fuelled environment at the top of the world's biggest financial services companies might have contrib-uted to the decisions that led to the 2008 financial crash.

One of the hurdles to any work in diversity and inclusion is that it relies on buy-in and support from the senior-most in the organization.

Arguably, people in these positions may have the most power to create change, but they may not have the empathic motivation.

The core group

In society, a 'power elite' – a small group of people at the very top of influential institutions (public and private) – essentially control a significant proportion of economic and cultural resources. This small group of people have the power to make decisions that affect everyone else in society. For example, in the United States, this includes highest ranking political leaders, army officers and large corporate CEOs. It is not to say that these people have intentionally formed a conspiracy but that it is natural for power to become concentrated in this way when such a handful of people hold such high authority in any group.

Similarly, in organizations, there is a power elite. This is what Art Kleiner calls the 'core group'.[3] This includes people in the senior-most positions but can also include some significant others, such as a big client or a trade union leader or a key local politician. It can also include employees who work in a strategically important division or who are part of a high-profile cross-functional team. Kleiner describes them as being the 'celebrities' of the company, the heroes, the people who are talked about, the people who have the power to get things done or to stop something from happening. Kleiner says that ultimately, all major decisions that an organization takes will be based on what serves the interests of this core group – not customers or employees or shareholders, as they may claim, but the personal interests of these few individuals. If this is the case, then, before you can make sense of who the organization is and how it works, you need to understand who the core group is and what their personal goals and priorities are, and how someone can (or cannot) enter or influence this group.

In one organization, an executive was selected to deliver a key project that had the direct sponsorship of the CEO and chairman of the organization. The executive and his work suddenly gained visibility in the organization. His work now required speaking to members of the board, holding corporate secrets, hearing political views and yet at times playing the role of a mute. He was expected to work without self-interest, holding confidences and demonstrating absolute loyalty to the aims of the organization, never taking sides. Yet he was also responsible for challenging senior leaders directly and confidently, without taking a position, recommending solutions (which sometimes went against the cultural norm or comfort of the organization), all in the long-term interests of the organization. The work directly served the need of the core group at the time when that organization felt it was under attack from external parties. The executive had become a trusted internal consultant at this critical time. The project came to a close and the executive was thanked formally by leaders and senior circles, who all knew him by name now.

The executive then returned to his 'normal duties' at his previous role and level, but his position in the organization had changed. He felt more 'looked after' in the organization than ever before. If he needed flexibility in terms of when, where and how he worked, he found that it was always available to him. When he needed time off, he always received it. There were occasions when HR rules were 'bent' to allow him to hire someone he wanted, and to maintain his bonus and long-term payments. When his family had personal security or health concerns, phone calls were made to ensure that the best doctors were made available or that protection could be ensured.

This may all sound like being 'made' in the fictional traditions of the U.S.-Italian crime syndicates or joining a secret society or clan. The sense that some people within organizations are more looked after, treated as special and have an invisible 'status' may not fit well with our egalitarian principles, but it is a reality of how things operate. The example of the executive is true and real, and it points to the importance of understanding who the core group is in your organization, how are they selected, what they value and what aspect of your work will motivate them so that change initiatives can be designed accordingly.

Without an alignment between the aims of the change initiative and the needs, interests and hopes of the core group, there will be little change for much sustained success.

The issue of diversity is intertwined with the issue of the core group because it is about who is in (or can ever make it in) and who is out of the inner circle, and who is listened to and who is ignored. For any subject on the table, if the core group decides it is important, it is and if they decide it isn't, then it won't be treated as such. For any diversity effort to work, it is imperative that the core group of the organization want it to. Culture change at an organizational level requires that enough people (in important enough positions in the company) genuinely want the change.

Most diversity experts assume that this means that what is needed is a strong business case. Yes, a business case is important. But that is not what we are talking about here. We are not talking about a rational understanding of why change is needed – we are talking about an emotional connection, a heartfelt desire, a personal empathy with the issue. Only once that is established for the core group in an organization, is it worth pursuing the question of how and what to change.

How decisions get made

What is important – and what is crucial when thinking about diversity and inclusion – is to have a clear insight into what the specific mechanisms are for decision-making within your organization. This needs to be examined on two levels:

1. *To understand* who *has decision-making power*: Most Diversity and Inclusion specialists are already doing this to some extent through demographically analysing role level by gender, age, etc., in order to see if certain types or groups of people are more likely to have power. This assumes, of course, that power is linked with position even though for some organizations, it might not be. Informal power and different forms of power also need to be taken into account, for example, if there are certain cliques or clubs or management favourites.
2. *To understand* how *decisions get made*: This is what is typically missing from the picture because it is not traditionally seen as an aspect of Diversity and Inclusion. What this means is taking a look at how information flows between different people and parts of the organization, how authority is granted, how many people are involved in decisions, what mechanisms are in place to ensure that employees

are making the right decisions (rule book, guidelines, close control by managers, committees, auditors, or trust?). What is the main basis for a 'good' decision? Taking a 'systems' view of the organization can help to shed some light on this.

Systems and networks

The modern organization is an organic, complex and interconnected web of people and places, where the sum is greater than the parts. The very fact that we use the term 'organization' acknowledges this, and invites us to take a view of organizations as 'systems', which have information flowing between its interconnected parts and a natural evolution taking place.

Systems theory studies the shape and set-up of a social structure in terms of how different parts of it are connected to each other. In ecosystems, elements such as air, water, energy, plants and animals work together to survive in a sustainable state, enabling each other and influencing each other. The same thinking can be applicable in the context of the organization. In an organization, for example, the different parts might be different departments, different locations, different types of employees, as well as external bodies (e.g. Unions) and technological systems that are inherent to the functioning of the organization.

Taking a systemic view of organizations is core to the practice of OD. To understand the working of a system, we need to look at the different parts – how they are connected and related, and how they work together – as well taking a step back from the parts and viewing the system as the whole. It is different from simply looking at an organizational chart because it includes informal power and not just roles, and gives a sense of actual working relationships rather than simply role relationships. It means looking at:

– What the main parts are, and how they are linked to each other?
– What are the inputs, outputs and processes in each part, and the system as a whole?
– Where are the boundaries, and what are they like: is it tight or loosely defined?
– What other systems does it come into contact with? How, when and where?

– Is it a closed system (independent of other systems and the environment) or open system (dependent on and connected with the external environment and others)?
– How can we improve the effectiveness and/or the efficiency of the parts and the system as a whole?

A systems approach can be very useful to solve problems when the organization feels 'stuck'. It involves taking a methodical and analytical view of the situation to analyse what parts are involved, what their roles are, and how processes and decision-making are playing out.

Network theory takes systems theory to a wider level. In systems theory, the unit of analysis is the system itself, and the workings within it. Network theory looks not only at how organizations function internally but how it links with other organizations and systems of the world and how these mutually influence and shape one another.

Network analysis helps to identify the key components of a social system, understand relationships and locate power within those structures. It helps us to gain a 'birds eye' perspective on how power is distributed and how information flows across the different lines, including where problems or conflicts may exist. In network analysis, we look at:

– What are the different parts of the network?
– Who are the key stakeholders inside and outside the organization?
– What is the nature of the relationship between these parts?
– How does information flow between these parts?
– Who has power? What are the 'nodes' where power is concentrated?
– What are the important and influential relationships?

It is more relevant than ever to understand networks in our increasingly complex, globalized and interconnected world, where information and power are accessed through multiple media and channels.

Systems and network analysis together help us paint a picture of the organization as a complex map of interconnected parts. They help us to quickly see where and how 'groups' of people operate in an organization, where unwritten rules might be operating based on informal power and how hidden structures and mechanisms might be contributing to (or hindering) optimal operational effectiveness. This helps us identify where power lies and who makes decisions and how. When you look closely at the culture, structure, power distribution and decision-making process within an organization, it should quickly become apparent where gaps are and why there may be a lack of diversity or a 'block' to greater inclusion in some parts.

Monkey theory

Sometimes, things get done in a particular way, because 'that's the way they have always been done' and no one has questioned why!

The 'Five Monkeys' study is often cited as a classic example of how organizational culture develops. The true source of this study (and whether it is actually a real study at all) is unknown, though it is sometimes attributed to the late Harry Harlow, a psychology professor at the University of Wisconsin. Nevertheless, it is a vivid example for how corporate cultures often evolve. This is how it goes:

Five monkeys are locked in a cage. A banana is hung from the ceiling and a step ladder is placed underneath it. One monkey starts to climb the ladder to reach the banana and immediately, all monkeys get sprayed with ice cold water. This happened every time a monkey tried to climb the ladder. Eventually they learned to associate the ladder with the ice showers and gave up trying to climb it. They had been trained into not reaching for the banana that hung from the ceiling and there was no need for the ice water showers anymore.

Then, one of the monkeys was taken out of the cage and replaced with a new monkey, who was not aware of the ladder–water association. The new monkey started to climb the ladder and the other four immediately pounced on him and beat him to stop him. They did this every time he tried, until he gave up, and learned that he should not try to climb the ladder or reach for the banana. (Note that there were no ice water showers any more.) The same happened when another monkey was replaced, and the replacements continued until the five monkeys now in the cage were none of the ones who had originally received the ice water showers. None of these monkeys had had the showers on them personally, or knew why, but they had learned that climbing the step ladder was not allowed – and not only did they follow the rule, they stopped others from breaking it, without knowing its reason or origin.

- Are there any example of 'monkey see, monkey do' behaviour in your organization?
- What is the reason for the behaviour?
- What are the consequences of the behaviour?
- Are we jumping on others to protect an outdated rule that is no longer helpful?
- What can I personally do to challenge this behaviour?
- What will make a difference?
- What kinds of changes to process (rewards/recognition/recruitment) will change the outdated and negative behaviour?

Summary

Organizational dynamics of structure, power, role and authority determine how things get done and how decisions get made. Decision-making is the smallest unit of organizational functioning and is a key aspect of Diversity & Inclusion because it drives who is listened to, who is included and what is valued. It is therefore important to understand who makes decisions and how they are made.

Systems and network analysis can be used to identify the interconnected parts within and outside the organization and map where power lies and where there may be blockages and opportunities for creating a more inclusive culture.

The most influential group in any organization is the core group. The emotional buy-in of the core group is a pre-requisite for any intervention to have traction in the organization. This is not just about presenting a rational business case but creating a personal, empathic connection for the core group with the value of inclusion.

---

[1] Smith, P. K. & Trope, Y. (2006). You focus on the forest when you're in charge of the trees: Power priming and abstract information processing. *Journal of Personality and Social Psychology, 90*(4), 578.

[2] Carney, D. R., Cuddy, A. J., & Yap, A. J. (2010). Power posing brief nonverbal displays affect neuroendocrine levels and risk tolerance. *Psychological Science, 21*(10), 1363–1368.

[3] Kleiner, A. (2003). *Who Really Matters: The Core Group Theory of Power, Privilege, and Success.* Random House, USA.

Chapter 10

External context

Chapter Outline

In this chapter, we look at the wider social context and its impact on organizations, and in turn the work of Diversity & Inclusion. We highlight the role of history, national culture and dominant ideologies, for example, the role of men and women in society. We discuss the importance of understanding cross-cultural differences and fostering greater appreciation of diverse perspectives in organizations.

The wider social context

Organizations do not exist in a bubble. The context (and by this we mean historical and social context) influences how we think about education, religion, politics, the economy, science and literature, and ultimately, how we organize ourselves and function as a group or society. These factors may exist outside of the organization but they have a powerful impact on how organizations work. Organizational functioning is influenced by local and global politics, international relations or war, religion and ideology. It is also affected by normative ways of thinking about different aspects of life, such as the views on the relative importance of money, medicine, nature or crime. Equal opportunities legislation was the original driving force for many current Diversity and Inclusion practices in organizations, in particular, monitoring representation and equal pay. Social context is complex and multifaceted, and often difficult to describe coherently as a whole, but it forms the background for the thinking and opinions of the founders of the organization as well as the current leaders. It drives what their primary concerns might be, what they are interested in, where they focus their attention and how they plan their futures, whether consciously or unconsciously.

Socioculturally there are histories, roles, stereotypes and power differences associated with different groups. These may be based on gender, class, caste, race, age, appearance, birthplace, accent, profession, where you live or other factors. These differentials colour the way we react and relate to each other at work, and they complicate the power differences that already exist in organizational hierarchies. So to understand the impact of difference in organizations, you have to first understand the context for these differences socially.

For example, talking about unconscious bias as a concept in itself doesn't mean much without an understanding of the dynamics in wider society that gave rise to certain stereotypes and biases. We have to ask where these stereotypes came from and what makes them negative or positive? Why do we make these automatic associations? Why do we value certain traits more than others? What is the historical, social, economic and legal context?

Many organizations currently have diversity statements about equal opportunities for Lesbian, Gay, Bisexual and Transsexual (LGBT) people. The tactical ability of a global organization to fulfil the promise of such a statement is significantly mitigated by the national, religious and cultural views of local employees, local legislation and longer-term economic interests for the corporation. Is it then valid for the global corporation to make a global promise? Taking culture and context into account might also mean being more open, honest and realistic about what can be achieved in a particular environment and working across the challenging intersection of organizational and local or cultural values.

Who is 'us' and who is 'them'?

In *The Second Sex* (1949), Simone de Beauvoir states:

> *No group ever sets itself up as the One without setting up the Other over against itself. If three travellers chance to occupy the same compartment, that is enough to make vaguely hostile 'Others' out of all the rest of passengers on the train.*

This would seem to be an anthropological truth about nations and groups of people, any grouping or creed of the human race. The 'lines' that we draw around who is 'us' and who is 'them' is based on where we are sitting and our current point of view. The lines then become seen as 'fact', and form the basis for protection, loyalty and belonging, and also for conflict, negotiation and war. This links back with our discussion on personal identity and group identity, where we make choices about who is our 'in group' and who is the 'out group'.

As De Beauvoir explains, 'in small-town eyes all persons not belonging to the village are "strangers" and suspect; to the native of a country all who inhabit other countries are "foreigners"; Jews are "different" for the anti-Semite, Negroes are "inferior" for American racists, aborigines are "natives" for colonists, proletarians are the "lower class" for the privileged'.

From Homeric poems to the *Sumerian Epic of Gilgamesh* and the *Histories of Herodotus* – our views of the world are grounded in social context created by those who record history, based on the position and perspective of the author, and who they see as 'us' and 'them'. More often than not, tales of war and the exploitation of the 'other' are given more attention than tales of peace, so these then become the basis for the collective history and identity of groups and societies. These narratives, based on difference and past conflict, become part of who we are, and they sustain ongoing hostilities between 'East' and 'West', Crusader or Ottoman, Christian or Muslim, or whoever is classed as 'foreign' or the 'other'. Historical and social narrative is built around the concept of *inclusion* and *exclusion* and this becomes our reality and our identity today.

Yet there is also an opportunity here to see past historical lines of difference and embrace our common humanness.

What joins one man to another in wider society is not common ancestry, language or race but the ability to feel emotions, to empathize and to share ideas and imagination. Our perceived lines of difference are old and traditionally presented a reason for conflict. Imagination allows us to create new possibilities about how we think about each other and challenge what are perhaps some of the most deeply ingrained aspects of culture.

Gender in the workplace

Let's take gender at work as an example. When women are treated in a certain way in wider society, this carries over into the workplace, where societal dynamics are mirrored. For example, if an organization operates within a culture that generally condones demeaning or exclusionary behaviour towards women (and these can be anything from sexist jokes to physical harassment, or restriction of the roles women can play in the society), these behaviours tend also to be treated less seriously in the workplace and this can have a strong impact on women's likelihood of entering (or thriving in) a male-dominated workplace.

Therefore, if we want to create a strategy to increase progression of women in a global organization, we need to first understand what role women play in the wider societies and communities, in each of the nations and cultures where the organization operates.

Sex role spillover

'Sex role spillover' is the term used to describe how gender norms, stereotypes and expectations for behaviour are carried over from wider society into the workplace, even when they are not relevant to the work. This is heightened when there is a skewed gender ratio. Male-dominated jobs get associated with stereotypically male characteristics, so 'activity, rationality, and aggressiveness' are emphasized.[1] In this context, females displaying the same behaviours are seen as an aberration from the norm.

Across many of our conversations with executives around the world we heard a common story: *A female executive had risen to the level in her organization where she was being considered by the board for one of the most senior roles in the organization. She was in competition with a male colleague. In the discussion, he was described as focused, direct, solution orientated or results driven. The same character traits in her were described as aggressive, bullying or combative.*

The nature of how men and women relate to each other at work, and how they are treated is a product of how society views men and women, their roles and the characteristics typically associated with each gender.

Masculinity and femininity

There is a lot of discussion in organizations and Diversity and Inclusion circles in particular about 'feminine' and 'masculine' traits in the way jobs are designed and workplaces operate. Stereotypes about women are sometimes used to explain why women may not progress in certain roles.

For example, in one meeting we attended, a research company was presenting some of its (fairly well-validated) statistics on 'male' and 'female' characteristics of jobs and matching these up with 'male' and 'female' ways of working. One aspect of this was differences in decision-making and thinking style. Women are typically seen to be more collaborative and therefore slower at decision-making, but more supportive, whereas men are seen to be more competitive and more decisive. Whether an organization values collaboration or decisiveness more might determine whether men or women are more likely to succeed in that environment.

Sometimes these characterizations are useful, as they may point to a traditionally 'masculine' way of operating (favouring competition over collaboration, for example) that acts as a barrier to women *and men* who think differently. However, these discussions can also perpetuate stereotypical ideas about women because not all women are collaborative and not all men are decisive.

Media and stereotypes

Gender and race are associated with powerful stereotypes, and yet, these categories are not fixed. They are social constructs that change with time and culture. *Gender* is culturally (socially) learned and adopted. It is not a biological reality like being male or female (although even the binary classification of physical sex can be challenged). Cultural ideas about gender are at the root of organizational ideas about gender. Similarly, conceptions of race and racial categories have changed over time and are a product of sociopolitical forces; they are not fixed categories with fixed characteristics and yet racial stereotypes are so strongly ingrained in most of us.

Where do stereotypes come from?

Stereotypes are created through history and culture. They are sustained and reinforced through media and images. You just need to pick up a few newspapers and magazine and look critically at the stories and pictures. How are different races, genders, ages, appearances, intellects, classes, countries and ideologies depicted in the newspapers and other media? What are the broad storylines and themes, how are the characters depicted, what roles do they play?

Similarly, we can take a critical look at company advertising. What images appear on ads of the company – both the ads to consumers and the ads to potential employees, as well as internal communications? Images in these media tell a story about how the organization sees itself as well as what assumptions it makes about what the target audience looks like or how the target audience sees itself.

Language creates reality

Looking critically means to also examine language, and ask:

- What words are chosen to speak about this subject or this person?
- What is the tone?
- What is not said?
- What is assumed?
- What are the underlying 'messages'?

It is impossible for us to think without the use of language and yet, language limits our thinking. The words we choose to use give meaning to our experiences and in that sense they *create* our reality.

Stories in the media, along with images and the use of language and tone, play a big part in shaping how we think and the stereotypes we

subconsciously adopt. These everyday messages are ultimately responsible for how we think about each other and what we see as normal and
good – both in our lives and at work. They affect what we see as important, what we value, where we spend our attention and what we ignore.
They affect what we see as right and wrong, good or bad, relevant or
irrelevant. Therefore, the media and visual images can be a powerful
vehicle for also countering stereotypes, shifting biases and creating new
associations.

In the next section, we propose that the use of media as propaganda is
a crucial part of creating cultural change and suggest ways in which this
can be done ethically and effectively.

Dominant discourses

Academics use a process called *discourse analysis*, which means taking a
critical look at the dominant ways of thinking and the dominant
scripts in society that shape the majority view. This means looking
around and asking questions about how society thinks and how it
creates meaning through language, and how it affects ways of thinking. Discourses are simply 'ways of talking about' a subject. But they
are not always neutral; they can be loaded with assumptions about
values, normality and power. A 'dominant discourse' is one that
becomes an overarching, normative way of thinking.

For example, think about how men and women are generally portrayed
in family structures on TV or in books and magazines, and even cartoons.
Of course there are exceptions, but generally speaking, what role and
position do husbands and wives have in stories, and what are the ideas
of 'normal' and 'good' we subconsciously adopt from what we see?

Motherhood

The discourse of motherhood is a good example. Think about how mothers
are portrayed in your popular national culture and what the characteristics of
the idealized mother are. This is different across different nations. This kind
of idealized portrayal of mothers occurs more frequently, and is more extreme

and more value-laden than the discourse of 'fatherhood'. As a result, being a 'bad mother' has stronger negative connotations than being a 'bad father', and this has a powerful impact on how men and women judge themselves and others, and make decisions. Discourses are not always neutral; they often create or perpetuate social inequality through language.

Now think about corporations and what images we associate with CEOs and board members. What are the dominant ideas about what leadership looks like in your organization, or how a successful manager behaves? What are the discourses around 'what it takes to succeed in this organization' or accepted ideas about what sort of people will eventually make it to the top? Who creates these discourses and how do they begin to dominate our thinking?

Dominant discourses are those that become widely accepted as 'normal' and 'common sense'. They are often created by people in power through the use of propaganda and intentional messaging and articulated through the culture of a place. They often reflect the perspectives and interest of the powerful groups. Movements like the Civil Rights Movement in the United States or the Women's Liberation Movement demonstrate a challenge to the dominant discourses of the time. Today, social media and the internet provide powerful vehicles to propagate both dominant discourses and the challenges to them.

Long hours culture

One dominant discourse in many organizations today is the idea of a 'long hours culture'. Sarah Rutherford highlights how this cultural assumption serves to exclude women from senior positions at work. She draws on Weber's idea of 'social closure'[2] to explain findings from her research into eight different company divisions.

Rutherford explains that 'time' is a commodity that we don't all have equal access to. Due to the way society is structured, women generally have more responsibility for domestic work and childcare, and men therefore have more access to time for work. So the only thing differentiating equally skilled and qualified men and women is their access to time, and this enables men to become more suitable for promotions. In this way, dominant (patriarchal) cultural discourses (like the 'long hours culture') can work to intentionally or unintentionally support groups that already hold power in organizations by maintaining the status quo.[3]

Once you have identified the dominant discourses and cultural assumptions in your organization or industry, you can critically ask:

- What impact does this discourse have on me, on my way of thinking?
- How does it affect the different types of people I work with or meet?
- What does it mean for men and women? Young and old people? Other groups?
- Does it really have to be like this?

Cross-cultural differences

We have used the word 'dominant discourses' interchangeably with 'cultural assumptions', because a key vehicle for the spread of discourses is culture. We refer to culture several times throughout the book. In this chapter, by culture we mean the wider societal or national culture, rather than the internal culture of an organization (although one affects the other).

Culture can be understood as a process that deals with the issue of how humans organize themselves and relate to each other and their environment. There are many classifications for understanding national cultures. One of the most popular is Hofstede's six dimensions:[4]

1. Power distance (hierarchy and power distribution)
2. Individualism vs. collectivism (whether personal or group needs are given greater focus)
3. Uncertainty avoidance (tolerance for ambiguity)
4. Masculinity vs. femininity (task orientation vs. people orientation)
5. Long-term orientation (how much importance is attached to the future)
6. Indulgence vs. self-restraint (how much people try to control their desires)

Another useful framework is one that was developed by Fons Trompenaars and Charles Hampden-Turner,[5] which has seven dimensions:

1. Universalism vs. particularism (*Whether rules are given priority or relationships/ circumstances*)
2. Individualism vs. collectivism (communitarianism) (*Whether individual needs or community needs are prioritized*)
3. Neutral vs. emotional (*Level of openness about feelings and emotions*)
4. Specific vs. diffuse (*The level of separation between the work and personal self, or the outward and inner self*)
5. Achievement vs. ascription (*Whether status and success is based most on who you are or what you do*)
6. Sequential vs. synchronic (*How time is viewed, and how much focus is placed on the past, present and future in daily decisions*)
7. Internal vs. external control (*How much control we feel we have over our environment*)

Such classifications can be useful for understanding cross-cultural differences within an organization. They help to interpret different ways of working, how things might be understood differently and why certain interactions and relationships might be smoother than others.

Trompenaars, in fact, goes one step further than just 'plotting' culture on these scales. He has applied the model in various business settings to help explain how cultural differences can lead to misunderstandings and conflict. He discusses how having an understanding of these differences can help organizations to reach a place of reconciliation. He says that diversity provides opportunities that are not often realized in organizations because despite rapid globalization and an increase in culturally mixed teams, 'our models or paradigms by which we view the world are still culturally biased'.[6]

Transcultural competence

In order to be truly global and truly local, multinationals need to foster 'transcultural competence' – the ability to reconcile differing values and viewpoints when we encounter a dilemma.

Multinational organizations need to avoid blindly 'universalizing' the company, based on the values of the parent company and they also need to avoid being too 'particularist' (e.g. having totally different systems in each country). They need to find a middle ground, which is based on an intelligent, inclusive, international approach. The first step to reconciling cultural differences is recognizing and respecting them. An understanding and appreciation of other cultures and cultural differences is a vital skill.

We need to actively develop and leverage existing 'trans-cultural competence' in employees – including (and especially) the senior-most. This is a key skillset for competitive aims in today's globalized world. Trans-cultural competence has two parts:

1. deepening specific cultural knowledge
2. developing our capacity to work across difference

The latter means developing our capacity to think in different ways than employees are used to, to be able to incorporate multiple viewpoints into any situation or dilemma and to be able to understand that there can be multiple equally valid and logical ways of analysing a problem. Having this ability helps us to get to a clearer, higher, multidimensional perception of reality, rather than looking at things in the usual or simplest way.

Developing cross-cultural competence is vital but it is no easy task and the 'clash' between cultures within organizations and between organizational and national cultures remains something we will struggle with for some time. In her book *International Dimensions of Organizational Behavior*,[7] McGill professor Nancy Adler asks to look at which is stronger: organizational culture or national culture and finds that it is the latter. With the exception of a few very culturally homogenous organizations (which recruit on the basis of cultural fit), working in multinational organizations actually heightens our national identity/ culture. So companies cannot assume that organizational culture will be able to supersede national cultural differences, and it becomes all the more relevant and critical to find a way to work across these differences.

A step to delivering cross-cultural competence is to look at existing models of leadership. Cross-cultural competence cannot be developed using a traditional top-down approach (command and control by a few senior people at the top) and neither with a purely bottom-up approach (where nobody comes together or takes a decision).

There is an opportunity to think about new models and language for leadership, which will be more suited to the multinational, multicultural and networked context in which we operate. One such new model is 'distributed leadership'.[8] This re-conceptualizes leadership as a process rather than a person, and highlights the importance of intentionally sharing authority to lead, depending on context. This means that the organization creates an environment where leadership (and followership) can flourish anywhere across the network. Such a model creates greater flexibility and adaptability for organizations operating in a diverse and complex environment and enables stronger, smoother working across difference. We talk more about leadership in Chapter 16.

Summary

In this final 'lens' we have highlighted the impact of the wider social and cultural context on organizations and individuals within it.

Social factors and dynamics are mirrored in organizations. We need to be aware of dominant ideologies and discourses, and how these affect our ideas of what is normal or good. We need to identify and challenge our cultural assumptions and stereotypes, particularly those that work to typify or exclude particular groups and maintain inequality. In Chapter 14, we outline a diagnostic guide, which includes key questions about the history and social context of the organization.

In addition to understanding our own culture, we also look across countries and societies to understand how different national and subcultures operate within our organization. We have to increase our understanding of cultural differences and develop our trans-cultural competence – our ability to look at situations from different perspectives – so that we can survive and thrive in a diverse and globalized world.

[1] Gutek, B. A., & Cohen, A. G. (1987). Sex ratios, sex role spillover, and sex at work: A comparison of men's and women's experiences. *Human Relations, 40*(2), 97–115.

[2] Social closure is a phenomenon whereby groups hold on to their power and resources by excluding others using different criteria, for example, private schools excluding those with less finances, or powerful membership organizations that rely on social networks. It is a way of explaining social exclusion.

[3] Rutherford, S. (2001). 'Are You Going Home Already?': The long hours culture, women managers and patriarchal closure. *Time & Society, 10*(2–3), 259–276.

[4] Hofstede, G. (2001). *Culture's Consequences: Comparing Values, Behaviors, Institutions and Organizations Across Nations.* Sage.

[5] Trompenaars, F., Hampden-Turner, C. (1997). *Riding the Waves of Culture: Understanding Cultural Diversity in Business.* Nicholas Brealey Publishing. London.

[6] http://www.tedxamsterdam.com/talks/riding-the-waves-of-culture-fons-trompenaars-at-tedxamsterdam/, Retrieved 15 January 2015.

[7] Adler, N. J., & Gundersen, A. (2007). *International Dimensions of Organizational Behavior.* Cengage Learning, USA.

[8] Western, S. (2013). *Leadership: A Critical Text.* Sage.

A Method for Change

Taking an OD approach

Chapter Outline

In this section, we propose a new, practical way to tackle the issue of Diversity & Inclusion at work. This addresses the critiques we outlined in Section 1 and takes into account the psychological, sociological and contextual perspectives we highlighted in Section 2. This approach is based on the premise that in order to create sustainable change in the area of Diversity & Inclusion, we have to work at two levels: we have to understand human behaviour and we have to tackle culture. One effective way to do this is to adopt an 'OD' or 'Organizational Development' approach. So, first let's briefly look at what we mean by OD in this context.

What is OD?

There are a number of definitions of Organizational Development or 'OD'. Most of these definitions are wide and vague and can really be understood to include any organizational effort that is aimed at improving its effectiveness, for example:

Organisational development (OD) is a deliberately planned, organisation-wide effort to increase an organisation's effectiveness and/or efficiency and/or to enable the organisation to achieve its strategic goals.[1]

Other definitions make more specific reference to the focus on people or the workforce – the human dimension of the workplace. For example, the Chartered Institute for Personnel Development (CIPD) in the UK offers the following:

> Organisation Development is about ensuring the organisation has a committed, 'fit for the future' workforce needed to deliver its strategic ambition. It plays a vital part in ensuring that the organisation culture, values and environment support and enhance organisation performance and adaptability. Provides insight and leadership on development and execution of any capability, cultural and change activities.[2]

Due to the breadth of its remit, there are a wide range of activities that potentially fall under the umbrella of OD and equally, there are a wide range of approaches and models and philosophical perspectives within OD. In essence, the focus of OD is on *human behaviour at work*.

Those who work within the area of OD are generally consultants in some form – either working externally or internally – to help examine and improve not *what* an organization does, but the *way* an organization functions. A big part of this is looking at the organizational make-up in terms of people, structures, ways of working and culture.

While OD is naturally linked with HR (both fields look at 'people' at work), they are not the same. HR professionals often find OD approaches confusing, unnecessary and too theoretical to be useful. This is because while HR is traditionally focused on the practical aspects of people management (processes and procedures such as selection, performance management, promotions, contracts, pay and holiday entitlement), OD is concerned with the less visible cultural elements (such as how people are organized into teams, the level of employee engagement or morale and ways in which decisions are made). There is an opportunity for more overlap between the working of OD and HR, through the strategic application of human behavioural principles to the practical implementation of policy and practice. One of the barriers to this is the nature of the OD profession, which can sometimes be 'inward' facing in terms of the language and methods used. Most OD consultants use a 'model' of culture or organizations, which can be seen to be either too academic or too over-simplified to have practical application.

In this chapter, we explain what we mean when we say 'take an OD approach' to diversity at work and offer some suggestions on how to make this work relevant and accessible to HR professionals and others working in organizations.

The use of models

A model can be an object, diagram or image that represents a subject, a process or a system being studied. Models help to communicate ideas, articulate processes and make predictions because models help make complex ideas easier to visualize.

OD professionals often use models to describe how aspects of an organization might function together. These models are normally rooted in psychological and/or sociological theories that have been tested and validated by academics, or they may be rooted in practice. Popular OD models include Schein's three-part structure of organizational culture, and Cameron and Quinn's dual axis classification, discussed in the earlier section. Many OD models tend to be simple 4 box diagrams showing two axes intersecting to create 4 'types' or straightforward linear models listing key properties. They may be based on data and analysis or on practical experience.

While an OD model might be well-tested and validated, they can never be perfect. Models in OD are inherently insufficient because they deal with human nature and culture, which is complex and cannot be reduced to a few bullet points or a set of four boxes. While the simplicity of a Venn diagram or a step-by-step model (such that the one described later in this section!) may be appealing, we must bear in mind that they can only ever act as a guide and not a formula. There will always be variations because each organization is unique and based in a different place and context. Models should not therefore be treated as universal solutions, because this is what leads to blind spots and missing what is unique, different, exceptional and possibly, most important to see.

The social context

It is also important to understand the social and historical context that a model or approach is based in. For example, in OD, models are created to explain culture. Culture is complex and potentially covers every aspect of what we can see (and what we cannot see) in organizations and groups. In order to be able to access this complicated concept, we need to simplify some of the key ideas within it into features or lists and create a way of capturing what is essentially shifting and intangible.

What we choose to focus on and how we choose to simplify a concept is based on our unique perspective, grounded in where we are in place and time and what we believe the purpose and nature of organizations is. This is often a reflection of societal trends in ideology.

Looking at the social and historical context helps us to understand why certain OD philosophies or theories might be practiced in organizations at a given time. They help us to take a critical perspective on why we adopt certain models and what the underlying cultural assumptions may be. Often, the theories we hang on to may be based in an outdated or no-longer-relevant conceptualization of organizations or society.

For example, Simon Western[3] discusses the concept of labour and leadership in organizations. He describes how our understanding of leadership has evolved with time, and how this reflects changes in society and economics. Multiple perspectives still coexist, often within the same organization, and this can challenge how we define and create a singular values-driven culture.

Discourses of leadership

Western describes four discourses, the first being the '**Controller**' discourse. This is based in the post-industrial revolution, particularly in the West, when machines were introduced to create a new type of workplace – factories. The need for more efficiency drove management thinking, and language reflected the machine metaphor of the organization (*toolkits*, blueprints, people are *cogs* in the system). This perspective was based on logic and efficiency and problems were tackled in a linear way. A key thinker and writer from this time was Frederick Winslow Taylor (1856–1915) who in his 1911 book *Principles of Scientific Management* sought to standardize, measure and reward work in pieces. Individuals' wants and needs, and diversity were not given importance, as the focus was on leaders *controlling* productivity and efficiency. This ideology still prevails in many industries and sectors.

The second discourse emerged after the Second World War. Western calls this the **Therapist** discourse. This perspective was born out of a desire to democratize, and to bring human decency after the horror of war. This era saw the establishment of 'welfare' as a concept in Western society, the creation of Health and Safety legislation, and the birth of Unions to help workers fight for their rights. Management theory began to focus on the psychological needs of workers: satisfaction, motivation and the opportunity for 'self-actualization'[4] of employees. Surveys were introduced to measure worker satisfaction and methods were deployed to prove the relationship between a 'happy worker' and a productive workplace. This thinking still prevails in much of management science, with the terminology having evolved from job satisfaction to 'employee engagement'.

The third discourse arose in the 1980s following the economic slump in the West and increase in importation and competition from Asian countries (Japan/Korea). Business schools and management consultancies became interested how leaders can *save* organizations from new competitors and the **Messiah** leadership discourse was created. Out of this came the 'celebrity CEO' on the covers of the business magazines, and the sense that a saviour executive could lead the organization out of difficulty. In wider society, figures such as Margaret Thatcher and Ronald Reagan were elected as decisive leaders, who were revered for their ability to make tough choices and create strong cultures, with an emphasis on loyalty and little tolerance of individual difference or speaking out against the culture. An interesting aspect at the same time was that Diversity & Inclusion practices were being introduced into many Western organizations. Viewed from a distance, these two ideas – Diversity and Strong Culture – oppose each other and yet were being executed at the same time in many organizations: celebrating difference (diversity efforts) and enforcing one consistent set of values that drive uniform culture (through strong leaders).

Western then promotes a fourth leadership discourse, which is currently emerging. He calls this the **Eco-Leadership** discourse. This draws on *networked thinking* in organizations. Networks reflect a (eco) systemic view of how people work together. Increasingly, in the modern organization, the matrix is chosen as the organizational principle. This means that people play multiple roles. For example, one may be accountable for the profit for a particular product in an organization and also be responsible for the performance of a geographically dispersed team. Work needs to be done in a way that integrates vertical and horizontal lines. It becomes increasingly important to look at linkages across and not just up and down the traditional organizational pyramid. This creates a new conception of leadership, as not just something that resides in one person (or a few people) at the 'top' but as being distributed across the network of the organization and potentially arising as and when needed.

Organizations today are more complex and global than ever before. There is a need for businesses and Organizational Development to adapt to the new social context we live and operate in.

The context today

New ways of work need new approaches from OD.

A world of networks

No longer do we have an expert craftsperson sitting at the centre, developing a product and taking it to the marketplace, guided by the practices of a master craftsperson or guild of experts. Today one team develops a concept, another team develops the marketing plan, different people build different parts of a product, others assemble it (often elsewhere in the world), and teams everywhere distribute and sell it in the market. Then there is a whole service industry, where there is no tangible product – it is just about concepts and relationships. With these modern ways of working, the social network between people (real and virtual) becomes increasingly crucial.

Lack of predictability

In Section 1, we referred to VUCA (a term used to describe the current geopolitical environment which is volatile, uncertain, complex and ambiguous). In a VUCA world, we need to be able to quickly respond and adapt our way of thinking and working, or we will be left behind. Having a diverse workforce and a flexible mindset is therefore crucial to being agile, relevant and competitive in this climate.

Taking a systemic approach

Systems thinking and network analysis, introduced in Section 2, provide a new way of conceptualizing organizations. In nature, systems thinking gave rise to our understanding of interdependence and the food cycle and ecosystems. In organizations, the systems consist of people, structures, the physical environment, rewards, work processes, finance, IT and other aspects. How well these aspects work together – and how well the organizational system engages with other systems (e.g. society, economy, politics) dictates how healthy, agile and efficient an organization will be.

Understanding the organization

Often HR practitioners or OD or business consultants arrive with a predetermined set of tools: a set of hammers looking for nails. Regardless of the issue, the same HR process tools are used again and again in different and differing organizations. We need to give more consideration to the uniqueness of each organization, the business conditions, the case for change and the culture – both the organizational and the external culture. This means paying attention to the early, diagnostic stage of the process, to truly understand the organization, before embarking on any intervention.

What we mean by 'an OD approach'

Coming back to the purpose of this chapter, what does OD mean and what do we mean when we say we need to take an 'OD approach' to the issue of Diversity & Inclusion?

What we consider important here is not to prescribe a particular perspective, or a certain set of models, but to highlight the general principles that underpin a good OD approach. These include:

- taking a humanistic and not a process view in trying to understand how people work together in organizations
- thinking holistically about diversity, rather than focusing on one aspect, strand or perspective
- seeing the organization as a system that has interconnected parts and that affects (and is affected by) other systems within its natural and social environment
- critically considering the social and historical context for how we think about human behaviour and organizations, and noticing dominant discourses at play
- using clearly thought-out models for conceptualizing organizations and cultures, which are not oversimplified and also not too academic to have practical use
- considering the role of the person in the organization, and taking into account the mosaic that each of us is individually and as a group
- taking context and culture into account, and not using a 'one size fits all' approach
- looking under the surface at the vast amount of information that is held within the unspoken, unwritten, understood ways of behaving and working in organizations
- creating sustainable, embedded change at the individual and organizational level

Summary

Organization Development (OD) is a field that applies an understanding of human behaviour to the workplace. A vital part of OD is examining culture and ensuring that there is an alignment between an organization's culture and its goals for the future. OD relies on the use of models which are inherently insufficient because they are dealing with human nature, and they are always a product of a particular historical and social context.

The view of the workplace and the individual worker has changed significantly in a very short span of time. Older and newer views are still both present in organizations. The world that we live in is increasingly complex, connected and volatile. Organizations in turn need to show flexibility and agility. This calls for a new set of OD approaches – and models. There is an opportunity for Human Resources departments to become more skilled in this area and apply more systemic approaches to working on culture.

In taking an OD approach, we highlight the importance of taking a holistic, networked and systems approach in understanding the role of people in organizations, and organizations in wider society. Human behaviour and the current social context must be taken into account in order to choose OD approaches that are relevant, effective and have the potential to create sustainable change at the individual and organizational level.

---

[1] http://en.wikipedia.org/wiki/Organization_development, Retrieved 30 January 2015.

[2] http://www.cipd.co.uk/cipd-hr-profession/profession-map/professional-areas/organisation-development.aspx, Retrieved 30 January 2015.

[3] Western, S. (2013). *Leadership: A Critical Text*. Sage.

[4] Self-actualisation is a term used in humanistic psychology. It refers to the fundamental human drive to find meaning and fulfil our personal potential.

Tips for consulting

Chapter Outline

Having set the scene for what an OD approach is, we now turn to the actual task of doing this work within organizations. This chapter addresses how you as a student, leader, manager or employee can prepare yourself for the process of consulting (either internally or externally) to initiate culture change in an organization.

The role of the consultant is important to consider because the success of any attempt to change something as fundamental as culture or to influence a group of people relies on the personal credibility, skill, style and position of the consultant, as well as their ability to really understand their own role in relation to the organization and their perceived 'fit' and purpose with the organization.

There are many models for consulting, most of which are presented as a step-by-step approach. They usually depict phases of the work, from the initial contracting and assessment, through to intervention and feedback, and are fairly intuitive and similar across most models. What we want to address in this chapter is not the process or the steps of consulting but some of the nuances of how it is done.

Preparing to consult

Listen and understand

Before anything else, your task is to listen, observe and understand the organization. This means looking at culture – both the visible and invisible aspects – to understand why things are the way they are, where the organization has come from, what is the real driver to change, who makes decisions and how. Once you appreciate the environment that you have entered, you can decide how to present and position yourself.

Build relationship and trust

In order to really engage with the key decision-makers or core group of an organization, and thereby have the best chance at influencing change, it is important to think beyond the steps and understand the *relationship*.

The analogy we use is the doctor–patient relationship. All doctors follow a consulting process. When you go to see a doctor, there are a couple of possible experiences. In both, the doctor is a highly trained professional, technically qualified and knowledgeable. In the first case, he or she asks you about your *symptoms*, makes notes and prescribes medicine. You get the medicine and the symptoms clear up, you get better. In the second case, the doctor asks you *how you are*. He or she seeks to understand other relevant aspects of your life, such as your job, your relationship and your hobbies. At the end of the conversation, you feel like they really know you. They prescribe the same medicine for you, but they also talk to you about life changes that may be helpful such as diet, exercise, work and habits. You listen and you accept what they say because you believe that they understand you and they have your best interests at heart. In both cases, you have a doctor who has the technical expertise necessary, but in the second case, they have taken the time to build a relationship with you, and to take a *holistic* view of you as a person, not just a body with physical symptoms. This makes you more trusting and more open to taking their advice on making changes aside from taking the medicine.

The type of consulting needed to help move an organization towards a culture of inclusion is akin to the second doctor. There is a need to engage the organization in things that they may not find pleasant to discuss, habits that they do not know they have and do not really want to change. For this, you need to work from a position of trust.

In fact, people are going to resist many of the things you might suggest. It will be easier to (and perhaps this lies at the root of the many of the current Diversity solutions) to look to simple process changes instead of sustainable systemic change. You need to demonstrate venerability, vulnerability and integrity, so that people in the organization can trust and respect you.

Know your intention
It is important to be clear about why you are doing this work:

- What is your personal purpose here?
- Do you know your personal motivation, and are you able to articulate it in a way that engages and inspires others?
- What is the personal story that brings you to this moment in a conversation with an executive or as an executive about to sponsor such work?

You are seeking to become a trusted advisor. This is a privilege. You must resist the temptation to allow ego and self-interest to cloud your work. You will have information that most people in the organization do not have. Keep your purpose in mind – why are you here and who are you acting for?

Be open
Think about the mosaic of who you are as you walk in the organization. You can draw on different aspects of your personal past to make connections and build relationship at different parts of the organization.

In this book we have intentionally shared personal stories from our lives. We believe that each time you share a story, you show an aspect of who you are and demonstrate your character. If you are transparent and honest about who you are, you open yourself up to the organization and in turn, invite the leaders and then the wider organization to open up to you.

Know your position

It is important to be clear about where you sit as the consultant in the organization. Are you 'external' or 'internal'? Are you already a member of the powerful core group, or are you connected to it? What is your personal power and authority and where in the network can you find this? Consider mapping out your own network to identify your key relationships. This goes beyond a normal stakeholder analysis. Think about the influence that each of your connections brings. What are their connections to each other? How will each of them view you in this new role? What does each of them need from you? Understand the power dynamics and relationships that are revealed in the map. This can help you identify points of opportunity or challenge.

Be the change you want to see

There is an adage in Organizational Development that the *process* of the change must reflect the *content* of the change. This means that the way the change is done should reflect the principles behind it. So if you are trying to build a more inclusive culture, then the process by which you do this on a day-to-day basis (project management, people management, behaviour, language, and personal values) must be inclusive.

Take a critical and open look at what words are used to describe the project or programme (and the cultural meaning of these words), what roles people play, who does what and how, how is the work managed, how is behaviour rewarded, what is prioritized, what are the timelines, what is the intent (stated and hidden), what are the struggles? Is there a disconnect between what you are trying to do and how you are going about it? If so, how do you resolve this? There may be some compromise to make in finding the balance between demonstrating new ways of working and not working 'against the tide'. You will need to find this balance depending on the appetite for change and risk, the timing and the context of your organization.

Have positive intent

All organizations have established networks and a 'normal' ways of doing things. An intrusive consultant will not go unnoticed, and is possibly under more scrutiny than others, because you are proposing change which automatically implies risk and threat to the status quo. To be accepted, you need to be able to show that you have a genuinely positive intent. You may need to reflect on and identify what you personally admire and respect in the organization and where your personal motivation comes from. Your words and intent, especially on something so personal as inclusion, need to be sincere. If this is not genuine, it will eventually show through and your efforts will be viewed with suspicion and possible rejection, regardless of how well you have crafted your change plan.

Engaging the core group

Every organization has a 'core' or 'elite' group which we make reference to many times throughout this book. The reason we have given this concept so much attention is because time and again, we have seen that no change is really possible unless it is aligned with the needs and interest of the core group. These are the key 'central' people in the organization who hold the most power and ultimate decision-making authority. It includes the senior-most, as well as others who may have influential power.

It is critical for the consultant to understand such dynamics in organizations and in wider society. Art Kleiner[1] demonstrates that marketing plans, spend, strategy, etc., are always driven by the interests of 'the core group'. The core group ultimately decides whether to start or stop activity, and their sponsorship and support is a pre-requisite for any change to be sustained.

A hierarchy is not a terrible thing in itself and logistically it is necessary for organizations that some (few) must lead. However, hierarchy can pose a challenge to this work because those who are in positions of power (and able to influence change) may be least motivated to do so. Core group members can be blind to aspects of 'groupthink' they are influenced by, and they may already be socialized to think in the way of the dominant ideology. They are likely to be more conservative towards change and in particular the introduction of new types of people (women, minorities, different world views, religions etc.). Having more power and authority can also reduce empathy and senior-most executives may be least likely to be motivated by the inclusion goals that will most benefit those who don't yet have power and position in the organization. The challenge, then, is how to create empathy, motivation and buy-in at the senior-most levels for this work on creating an inclusive culture. This is not just about presenting a rational business case, but creating emotional buy-in: Why should they care?

Initiating change

Culture 'change' as risk

Using the word change can sometimes bring up resistance. If you are an executive, part of your role is to protect the organization from revolution and manage risk. Change of culture is significant risk. So how do you, as consultant, position yourself so you are not seen as posing a risk to be avoided? Avoid using the words culture and change in the same phrase too often.

Any attempt to influence a culture must be built on the foundations of the existing historical culture, with careful consideration of pivotal interactions with the external environment.

Cultural systems are largely self-referential; in order to influence forward movement within the culture, you have to first understand and work from the current place and use the methods that are currently culturally acceptable. The unique values, deeply rooted beliefs and institutional memory of a company are not easily erased. Periodically a culture needs re-articulation, re-enactment and re-positioning to continue to be relevant. As the consultant, you have to show respect to the current culture and values and understand why they may be the way they are. You have to be aware that you may be seen as a potential threat if you rush in to change something before you have understood it or if you use an approach that meets with immediate rejection because it clashes too strongly with existing values.

Burning platform vs. strategy enablement

Many change approaches speak of the need to articulate the so-called burning platform. This language comes from the work of John Kotter,[2] who developed an eight-stage process of creating change, which begins with the need to create the perception of urgency.

The idea was that organizations need to be seen to be 'on fire' – a real sense of urgency – to create the impetus for change. This approach seems very dramatic and potentially explains the frantic search for metrics to build a business case for diversity. We have heard too many diversity professionals claiming *that if only we could get the right causal data and make it very solid – then the case for change would be strong enough and 'they' would do something about it.* This mindset has placed Diversity practices in perhaps an unwinnable position – never creating the impetus for systemic change.

Organizations make big changes all of the time. They enter new markets, develop new products, attract new segments, change CEOs and so on. This is called execution of strategy. Strategy and subsequent execution (i.e. change management) is a normal process of organizational functioning and not always driven by a perception of being 'on fire'.

For any work on culture and diversity to have sustainable impact, it must be tied to the strategy of the organization. The senior team needs to see this work as being tied with what they are trying to do commercially and they need to have realistic expectations of what changes to expect and when. The role of the consultant is not 'selling' the solution but making linkages between the strategy and culture so that it becomes integrated into what the organization already does. A number of departments will need to work together to be able to co-ordinate the work (not just HR). This requires a total enterprise view that enables different functions to cooperate and work towards a well-understood, common strategic goal.

Aside from understanding the stated strategy, it is also important to understand the inner (sometimes-unarticulated) hope that the executives of the organization have for the organization. Once the consultant understands the hope that the organization has for itself, it becomes easier to begin a journey of inclusion that is genuinely aligned with that hope. An inclusive culture is something that must first be imagined as something we all hope for, and the most important role of the consultant is to *inspire that hope* in the hearts and minds of the key members of the organization.

Dealing with resistance

Each organization has 'white blood cells', 'antibodies' that will detect a change in the organizational system – this will attract attention. Some will join the change, some will come to look because they are curious and some may try to sabotage it. It is much easier to find those who are passionate and leverage their passion rather than trying to convince the negative few to be otherwise.

When people come to join the project, they may want to own it independently or run it locally. As long as this doesn't do any harm or run counter to the values of the work, it is important to encourage this initiative and allow it to flourish even if it means relinquishing some control over the work. This is how you can create passion and contagion, an easier task than fighting resistance.

Your role as consultant

Consultant as court jester

The outside-in perspective is often missing in organizations and this is part of the role of the consultant. In the story of the Emperor's Clothes, a small boy in a crowd is the only one that can see and say that the Emperor has no clothes on. For the consultant attempting to work with culture, the experience can be similar, being the only one who can appreciate that things are not what they may seem on the surface. We often say 'Fish can't see the water'.

In the old medieval courts, the Jester/Fool/Clown was the only one who could sometimes speak truth to power in this way without fear of punishment. They served not simply to amuse but to criticize their master or mistress and their guests. Queen Elizabeth (reigned in the UK, 1558–1603) is said to have rebuked one of her fools for being insufficiently severe with her. At times the role of the consultant is to play the 'fool' at court, to be the only one present who has no political agenda and is capable of speaking total truth to power, sometimes directly and publically.

The external perspective is valuable to the organization, but the organization will be wary of outsiders who ask difficult questions or make seemingly negative observations because they disrupt the normal way of thinking. People need to see you not as a threat, but as a facilitator, who is there to help and to guide by (respectfully) shining a light on those aspects which may be hidden from view to everyone else around.

Use yourself as an instrument

You should treat yourself as if you are a thermometer or weather vane, and pay attention to how you feel. Once you separate out the purely personal (e.g. if you're having a bad day because you didn't sleep well or if you are having personal problems), very often, the feelings and moods you experience can give important clues about how an organization works and how it impacts people. Your emotional and cognitive reaction to something is real and could indicate how others in the organization also feel, but may not have the detachment to be able to point out why. So, be mindful of your own reactions and take the time to try and understand what triggers them, when and why, and what this possibly tells you about the organization. If appropriate, share this with others to try and understand whether it may be indicative of something in the environment that needs to be addressed.

The process of change

Every management book or theory, including this one, attempts to explain the process of change in the form of a step-by-step model. Models have become modern organizational shorthand for making the complex simple and they give the practitioner a sense of control and order, in a journey that is inevitably chaotic.

Applying the approaches traditionally used in change management may not be as neat as the models imply. Once the process of change starts, a wide range of factors determine how things pan out and what happens next. The appetite for change, the speed and pace, the process and how it is managed varies radically, depending on the nature and the culture of the organization. It is an organic process that is affected by a wide range of external factors. The plan must take account of this vulnerability and build in the required flexibility and adaptability needed to fit the organizational context over time.

Speed of change

The speed of change is a choice and reflects the nature of the business strategy. In some cases, the strategy seeks immediate results in a short span of time – months or annually. In others, strategic plans span several years. The nature of strategy and how far out it is thought through is itself an example of the culture of the organization, which reflects industry and national history. Different ethnic and national cultures also work at different time horizons. Truly changing culture takes years.

It is important to take into account how quickly the organization is accustomed to seeing 'results' and manage expectations. You may need to make a proactive decision about realistic short- and long-term aims. Often, the sponsor in the executive team will be used to working on a shorter corporate timeframe, and will want to see some results by quarter or by year-end. It may be helpful to 'chunk' the work into manageable bits that fit into shorter and longer timeframes. Expectation management is part of earning trust. For many who seek to influence significant change, the results are not always seen in their lifetime with the organization, instead they put the 'seed's of change in place with the hope and knowledge that if done well, the process will work over time.

Establishing governance

Be careful not to establish governance of culture too early. It is tempting to put a formal change/communication plan together straight away because in most organizations, project plans are how things get done. For some specific task-related issues that need an execution focus, a plan may be necessary, but there also needs to be some space for the new way of thinking to emerge and evolve organically.

As expectations and norms slowly shift, previously acceptable behaviour will perhaps no longer be acceptable. Some leaders and managers may continue to use language or reflect views that are now seen to be 'counter-cultural'. In these instances, it is important to remain neutral and facilitate the organization to work through how to deal with deviance from the vision. You have to help the organization to figure out for itself how to think and act differently rather than them relying on you as the consultant to give them the answers.

Summary

This chapter addresses the role of the consultant in an OD approach to culture change: how the consultant prepares for entry into this work and the importance of the relationship with the organization.

While change models offer the pragmatic 'how to', ultimately, the success of any change initiative depends on the perceived trust, credibility and genuineness of the consultant. To be effective, any consultant – whether internal or external – needs to demonstrate that they have the best interests of the organization at heart, and that they can be trusted. They need to manage expectations, and relate the work they are doing to the strategic goals and the interests of the core group in the organization.

---

[1] Kleiner, A. (2003). *Who Really Matters: The Core Group Theory of Power, Privilege, and Success.* Random House, USA.

[2] Kotter, J. P. (1996). *Leading Change.* Harvard Business Press. Boston, MA.

Chapter 13

Introduction to the iterative model

Chapter Outline

The six lenses discussed in the previous section provide a diagnostic framework to help understand the precursors of Diversity & Inclusion. In this section, we look at how to apply those ideas in creating a tactical solution.

A strategic and tactical approach

One of our key critiques of current efforts in the field of Diversity is that they are not planned strategically and not structured in a way to maximize impact. Efforts are often focused purely on process, or metrics, without sufficient consideration given to other aspects of behaviour change. A new approach is proposed in this section. It is a tried and tested, practical method for addressing the issue of diversity through a series of steps that work iteratively to instigate and embed cultural change in organizations.

It is a strategic Organizational Development (OD) approach that has the following characteristics:

1. *Holism*: As demonstrated in the causal model in Section 2, there are a wide range of factors that affect culture, so these need to be addressed holistically by taking different perspectives and ensuring that the programme is not narrow in focus or rooted in one philosophy or way of doing things.
2. *Congruence*: It is important to consider congruence across initiatives and between the work and the overall organizational strategy in order to minimize disconnection and dissonance. The work has a greater impact when the different aspects are aligned and integrated.
3. *Sequence*: The order in which interventions are introduced matters, and can make a difference to the impact of the programme as a whole, so the sequencing of steps and stages needs to be thought out.
4. *Imagination*: Triggering the imagination is a crucial first step to creating any change at the individual or organizational level. What we see affects what we believe and what we believe creates hope and reality. The mind's eye is the crucial starting point.

Being holistic

Current approaches are often dictated and motivated by the perceived 'best practices' of other corporations, or by legislation, pressure from groups with different interests, what is seen as the latest management consulting trend or the latest article from a leading business school or think tank. Interventions can be disparate, and there is often a lack of cohesive, strategic action over time. This in part has mitigated real progress.

Putting a 'band aid' on a diversity problem through the use of a new target or rule may help to shift the needle temporarily, but it doesn't resolve the underlying cultural issues that may be responsible for the current state. Sending women onto a women's leadership programme, even if facilitated by the best business schools that budgets can afford, will have little long-term impact in creating a sustainable culture for how women feel, are treated, recruited, promoted and succeed in the organization.

There is an opportunity here to shift the paradigm for how we consider the issue of Diversity & Inclusion, and move it from its place within HR process to becoming a strategic and commercially driven approach that is seen to be integral to business strategy.

Being holistic makes the task much more complex and difficult (which is why more tokenistic approaches are generally implemented) but it is absolutely necessary in order to move out of our current stagnation in diversity practice.

Being congruent

The issue of congruence is also critical from a stakeholder perspective. Employees are cynical about the same old rhetoric of Diversity & Inclusion because it is often viewed as 'just talk' or 'ticking the boxes', and usually only extends to small, short-term measures that may be seen to be tokenistic, and which do not lead to any significant felt change in 'how things are'.

Congruence means consistency between what is being said and what is being done across the organization. This extends not only to the stated policy (we all have equal opportunities policies), but to real practices in all areas of organizational functioning. Congruence means embodying the principle of inclusion not only in HR processes (reward, recruitment, promotion, etc.) but in what is valued and rewarded (explicitly and implicitly), how people are treated (whether they are employees, customers or suppliers) and in how the organization conducts all of its day-to-day business.

When there is congruence, employees start to have more faith because they can see that there is no disconnect between what is promised by executives and the reality of their work experience. This confidence and trust also extends to other stakeholders (media, regulators, shareholders, customers, prospective customers and prospective shareholders), and then becomes part of the brand – something that the organization is known for – and when the brand is powerful, it is intertwined with culture. Having congruence in articulated values and visible practices across the organization is crucial in maintaining both brand and culture.

Congruence also means consistency with the overall strategy. Strategy encompasses the idea behind what we are trying to do and why, and how it fits in with the overall purpose of an organization. The push for change can come from a range of sources, based on what the organization has to do in the short, medium and long term. The business case (the impetus for the work) needs to be based on a clearly articulated link between inclusion and the strategic objectives and purpose of the organization. Some examples of this are discussed in Chapter 17.

An iterative approach to culture change

The iterative approach, which is proposed in this section, seeks to take account of the whole system in a phased way. It considers the commercial strategy, the mindset change required and then the policy, systems, people processes, governance and behaviour required to sustain the culture for the long term. We call it iterative, by which we mean the order is intentional and important, and one stage leads on from the last.

We propose six broad stages.

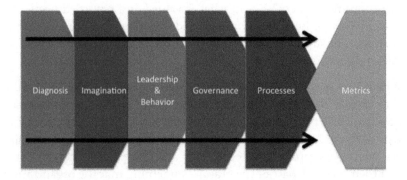

While we hope that these six steps provide a clear framework to base a tactical approach on, we want to be clear that we do not consider this to be a universal solution. You will need to adapt and fit this to your organization and context. This framework is provided as a starting point, based on our experience.

You may also need to make other subtle adjustments, for example changing the terminology or depiction, to suit your audience and stake-holders. You may need to re-draw these steps in the form of a spiral, a ladder, consecutive circles or images, depending on how information is best understood and communicated in your context. These may seem like trivial changes, but the way information is presented can make a difference in whether and how well it is understood and accepted. Different organizations have different preferences in terms of how information is presented and what is seen as the best way to get a message across. This preference is also an aspect of diversity – it shows how the organization's leaders evaluate information, what is considered valid and important, and what styles of thinking are favoured.

On one occasion, I worked with a consultant who created a change plan for a leader in our organization. It was very well thought-out and included the formal phases of a quite complex change that the organization was undergoing and he had mapped these like a 'mind map', showing the phases, linkages, stakeholders and resources required. The response was negative. The leader said that they did not understand the approach and that it was too complicated and unclear.

A colleague reviewed the material and suggested that all of the same material be put into a linear box grid and reformatted into how the organization typically presents material. This was done and the same material was presented, one week later. The response was significantly more positive. The consultant was praised for his understanding of the complex organizational process.

It is also worth bearing in mind that in reality, change never takes place in this neat and simple way. There is often re-ordering, going backwards and forwards and overlap of phases along with emergence of unplanned events which dictate how the change really unfolds. So the six steps are a rough guide for what is invariably a complex journey.

The six phases

We propose the following broad 'phases' for the work, which provide a framework:

1. Diagnosis
2. Imagination
3. Leadership and Behaviour
4. Governance
5. Process (HR and Business)
6. Metrics

Diagnosis

The initial work is diagnosing where the organization is, and where you want to be. Before we begin the change process, we look at the present situation and context of the organization, and try to understand the key factors at play, both historical and current. How things work and how change takes place in every organization is different. We find this out by asking questions, not just about the diversity statistics but about the history and normal practices of the organization, how things get done, the strategic direction and hopes. We then work to convert the strategy into a plan of action.

Imagination

This is the first step to kick-start a mindset change. We trigger the imagination about what is possible and articulate collective hope. This stage is about using communication, media and stories to positively and ethically articulate and support the aspiration and strategic direction.

Leadership and behaviour

We then look at how people behave (and how they change their behaviour), and in this context, the impact of leadership. We pay attention to creating leaders and building leadership practices that will sponsor and role model the behaviour desired. We believe that focusing on leadership doesn't only mean training the senior-most people, it means building the capacity for strong leadership across the organization.

Governance

Governance is about creating formal sponsorship, policies, procedures and mechanisms that support the culture change process.

Process (HR and other)

In the process stage, we look at how activity in different areas impacts (or reflects) the culture. This includes 'people' practices such as hiring, on-boarding, promotions, reward, performance management, and exit – the whole employee life cycle. It also includes other day-to-day business practices such as sales, marketing, budget/planning and any other activity, to understand how it impacts employees and stakeholders.

Metrics

This is a familiar area for most of us working in Diversity and Inclusion. 'Metrics' is where the work usually begins and ends and remains focused. Metrics are a crucial part of any plan so that we can measure where we are. Measurement is necessary but measurement alone is not a strategy and we put this towards the end of our iterative approach.

There is also an opportunity to expand the use of metrics to measure not only visible aspects of demographic diversity (and use them as indicators of equality and inclusion) but also to measure cultural indicators.

The last three phases of the above model are where the work of Diversity currently resides – but we propose that the first three stages are crucial in enabling the process changes to have sustainable impact.

Summary

This chapter introduces our approach to tackling Diversity & Inclusion. We highlight the key characteristics of our approach: taking a holistic view, being congruent and strategic, being intentional about sequence and using imagination to trigger mindset change. Change is necessarily emergent and will vary across organizations, but we have outlined six stages that offer a framework and starting point. Much of the work that is detailed in these stages may already be taking place in organizations. It is the nuance of making linkages, sequencing, timing and intent that creates a recipe for success. The chapters that follow expand on each of the six phases.

Chapter 14

Diagnosis

Chapter Outline

Much like in medicine, a thorough diagnosis and understanding of the 'patient' is key to selecting the right 'treatment'. Getting this wrong, or lack of care in truly understanding the problem, the context and the needs, may result in a short-lived or ineffective solution.

Understanding the organization includes understanding the culture. Culture is what defines organizations, and drives many other aspects of how it functions. It is what keeps the organization together and maintains its unique identity. When taking an OD approach, the first essential step is to examine and understand the culture of the organization you are working with and make an assessment of 'where we are' and 'where we want to be'.

Using the causal map as a diagnostic framework

The causal map outlined in Section 2 of this book can provide a diagnostic framework to help make sense of current patterns. The six lenses provide different perspectives on any diversity problem, and together they will help to paint a realistic and holistic view of the current situation.

For example, if you are looking to understand why there is low representation of women at senior leadership in your organization, there are different ways you can explain this.

- From the perspective of personal identity, you might ask: Do women fail to identify with leadership or the organization after a certain point? Do other people make incorrect assumptions about the role and nature of women in these positions?
- From a cognitive perspective, you can look at the possible impact of unconscious bias against females or the use of a limited range of decision-making styles.
- From a cultural perspective, you can attribute the disparity, at least partly, to social gender roles and norms.
- From an organizational perspective, you can look at the history and industry of the organization, where it was formed and with what aims, where women feature in this, and how business is done.

Culture is everything

One of our key principles is taking a holistic rather than a narrow perspective. So when we consider organizational culture, we must take into account the 'formal' aspects (such as the stated values, mission statement, structure) as well as the informal or implicit aspects. *Everything* in the organization is a manifestation of the culture: the way that the budget is completed, the manner of the IT function activity, the types of uniforms worn, the colour of the wall, all of these create culture. So when you are in the diagnostic stage, your task is to be curious and notice every detail of how an organization appears and functions.

You need to look not only at the visible aspects of culture, but also the unwritten ways of working and the unspoken assumptions. Even seemingly trivial details might tell you something about how the organization ticks.

Upon entering one organization I was assigned a personal identification number. That number was linked to my email address and security tag, and gave me access to the organization generally. I commented at one meeting with executives that they did not have the 'number' assigned to them, and I learnt that past a certain organizational level, you are known by name not number. Senior executives were able to maintain their personal identity while the rest of the organization were treated (like the army or penal systems) as a mass and anonymous entity. The number removed identity and also showed rank. This small observation brought insight about an underlying philosophy about position and power in the organization.

Totems as guides

Part of this task is to look for what we call 'totems'. Historically, totems refer to spiritual symbols (objects or emblems) that held cultural meaning and served as a reminder of a group's ancestry or history and which became symbolic of the group's identity.

Organizations have totems, too. Looking for the 'totem' means identifying the important symbols and stories that create cultural meaning in the organization. Totems help to explain: what is important to people here, what is this company about?

We worked with one company that deals with delivery of mail and material, often in hazardous or challenging conditions. Their motto is about delivering at all costs, and this is what they had become known for externally. One of the key core competencies for all employees was what they referred to as 'execution focus' and there were stories being told among employees about other employees who had managed to beat the odds and deliver something on time under very challenging circumstances. Such employees were heralded as 'heroes' for their commitment to on-time execution. Solutions that were 80 per cent complete ahead of schedule were rewarded more than those that were 100 per cent but missed a deadline. Failure to achieve a deadline meant career suicide. Being late for a meeting was unacceptable. Clocks were visible everywhere. The clocks, the motto, the competencies and the stories are all totems that help us understand what is really important here – time.

At the diagnostic stage, your role is play detective: to understand what the key totems are and to then design and conduct the change work in a way that is aligned with how the organization ticks. On some occasions, the totem itself may be part of the issue that requires attention and will require a deft touch to show why.

Immerse yourself and talk to people

The best way to understand a culture is by immersing yourself in it. Spend as much time as possible with the people in the organization – walking the floors. Don't just visit the boardroom and offices but also the shops, hubs, factories and call centres. It is important to walk in the shoes of the different people who make up the mosaic of the company.

For example, spend a day with an area manager, in her car, asking questions about what her life is like and spending time with her in her meetings finding out what she does: who are the other departments that she meets with, how is she rewarded, who does she manage; how big is her team, what has her career trajectory been like; can she name the CEO; what is to her the most senior level of the organization (often people may perceive a middle manager as having ultimate authority, or being as important as the Group CEO, and it is interesting to understand why). There is one always-important question in this phase: *if you could do anything, fix any one issue what would you do?* This should be done at many levels and in different parts of the organization.

Look for stories and examples

Try to get an insight into overall themes but also subcultures and the range of different views across the organization. Identify places to look for examples and stories to help you paint a complete picture of the organization. Identify gaps in your understanding, and speak to people who can fill these gaps with their personal knowledge. Knowing personal and local stories and examples will also to give you credibility when you are able to recount a local detail or example to a member of the senior team. You are acting as a 'story collector' for the organization to help it to create its own identity. We talk more about the power of story-telling in the next chapter.

A diagnostic guide

Here are some aspects to pay particular attention to when diagnosing an organization:

1. **What is the history? What is the context?**

How did this organization come to be? How, when, where and why it was originally founded? What was the national culture where the organization was first established and where it now operates? What was the social, political and economic context for its formation?

What has the organization been through? Who were the important leaders and what were the key decisions in the history of this organization? When did the organization face a challenge and how did it emerge? Knowing the organization well accelerates your acceptance and ability to influence. To do this well, find an old trusted advisor, possibly one of the elite who is close to retirement. Ask for their mentorship, and take the time to listen to their stories.

Look at history, then look at the present.

What is the current context: operating conditions, competition, market demands and societal trends? What is the political and economic climate? What are the national cultures that influence the thinking here? What are the current dominant discourses in this organization and where do they come from?

Most importantly, are the present-day practices supporting the kind of culture that the organization needs in order to continue to thrive in today's context?

A major global financial services company had become known for being extremely risk-focused and prudent. These are traits that are highly valued in traditional banking and they are a reflection of the values of its 'founding fathers' at a time when financial security was a top priority for most people.

The same values remain core to the behaviour, practices and success of the financial services organization today. It was these traits that were deemed to be behind the resilience of the financial services organization during the economic downturn.

Yet, as time passes, the same traits are no longer as critical as they were. Security and prudence is still necessary, but this has to be balanced with innovation, an agile response to competition and delivering unique customer service. Due to the basic risk aversion in the company, the organization became slower to respond to external events and trends. It was behind the competition on new products and less responsive to customer demands for new ways of banking. The same trait that put it ahead of the competition was now turning into a competitive disadvantage.

The culture changes daily as new people join and contribute to the organization. With intent, bits of the history that you want to exemplify can be carried forward while also imagining and developing new ways of doing things.

2. Who is in this organization?

This goes beyond looking at the number of employees and percentage of males, females, etc., at different levels. You also need to think about multiple layers of identity beyond the main equality strands. What are the different groups and perspectives present, what different personal histories and backgrounds do people bring, and how do different groups coexist and operate together in this particular context.

Identify the different aspects of personal and collective identity that are relevant as well as the critical points of difference and diversity, and how they interact. What social groupings and cultural dynamics are reflected here? Think beyond the main equality strands.

Think of the person in the organization

The organization is a mosaic of individuals, and each individual is themselves a mosaic of the different aspects of their personal identity and affiliations: age, gender, ethnicity, religion, marital status, sexual orientation, social background, language, history, physical appearance, geography, work role, communication style, leadership style, self-perception, self-confidence and ways of working.

The type of the business will also impact the nature of the people who work in the organization. What type of competencies and qualifications does the organization emphasize? Are people here mostly engineers, scientists, bankers, academics, sales people or artists? What is the typical educational and social background? How does this professional view impact the culture and the way things are done?

Think about the dominant groups and the different types and *segments* of employees. Any categorization will be limited, but taking into account as many layers as possible of personal identity and lines of difference will paint a richer picture of *who* the organization is. What is the gender, age, tenure of each different segments? What do they want from the organization in general? What does this segment bring to the organization? For an OD consultant trying to understand how an organization ticks, it is important to have knowledge of the diversity and uniqueness of who it is that comprises the organization and how *they* tick.

3. Where does the drive for change come from?

Why have you been called in? Who has asked for this work to be done? Is it the CEO/Chairman? Has the board put pressure on the executive officers to amend some aspect of the diversity of the organization, or to fix a particular issue in the female pipeline? Is there external pressure, for example from something in the media or changing legislation?

Who are your supporters and why are they looking for change?

For the person who is key sponsor, what is the personal story for them that makes this work important?

What is the broad motivation for this work: must, need or want?

4. What exactly is the aim?

There is often a difference between what is expected by the organization and what you, as the consultant, think needs to be done. You will need to understand what the different stakeholders really imagine and expect and make decisions about whether, when and how to deliver a holistic and systemic plan. Very often, the stated goal of diversity projects is very narrow, for example to increase representation of women in senior levels to x per cent. It will be your role to think about how to manage and negotiate targets like these in the wider context of organizational change and demonstrate to your stakeholders the importance of taking a wider, holistic approach.

5. What does 'good' look like?

What is the collective aspiration for this organization and how can it best be articulated? What does the ideal behaviour look like? In Chapter 17, we discuss how process and formal systems can help to codify these behaviours into formal competencies, systems and processes. At this stage, it is about identifying what the ideal state is and how it can be visualized and described in a way that everyone understands, feels inspired by and can apply in their daily work.

6. Are there examples of where this is already done well?

We will talk in the next chapter about the process of Appreciative Inquiry. This is a critical method to collect and articulate real life examples that capture the collective aspiration of the organization.

Listen for examples and stories that you can share, particularly those that show where the organization has already has done some of the things being proposed or where things have worked well. You are then able to present the change as something that has already been done and has been proved to be effective, rather than something new and daunting. In one organization, I heard someone recount a story about how a CEO had moved a mid-level manager from India to China in the late 1800s. This had been presented as a 'social experiment' at the time, and was accompanied by a note from the CEO that 'every effort of politeness should be taken to ensure that the experiment worked', in other words, that the transition would be smooth. I was able to use this story from over 100 years ago to show the organization why a mid-level managers international rotation programme should be funded today – that this is grounded in how the organization has always done things. Senior leaders in the organization's past had set a vision for diversity that was rooted in their history.

7. Where is the passion?

Many people feel inspired by this kind of work and they may reach out because they want to be part of the positive future. Identify, welcome and embrace this. Building on passion where it originates is a way to set up contagion and momentum for change. Consider how they can be a positive part of the change being planned in the context of their work.

Often, the areas that will pick up change fastest will not be in the HQ building. They will be at the 'edges' of the organization, where they are not under the direct sight of the senior leaders. Often the case for an inclusive culture and what can be done will resonate with the edge before the centre because they need it more and will be able to apply it directly and immediately to their work. Allow this and bring these stories back to the centre for inspiration. Find your allies in the external edges of the organization and celebrate their progress and passion.

8. What and where is the sponsorship?

Sponsorship looks different in different organizations. You, as the consultant, can never be the sponsor. Sponsorship in some companies looks like role modelling; sometimes it means giving funds, permission, resources and instructing departments to comply. Sometimes it is giving a speech or clearing political roadblocks. Think carefully about what unique sponsorship may be required for each stage, and what it may look like in your organization.

9. How do things get done? How do decisions get made?

What are the important structures and processes here, and how do decisions get made?

It is necessary to create the case for change in the *manner* in which the organization currently operates. In some organizations, which are rule-driven, decisions and changes are made by writing new policy, or guidelines. In other organizations, it might mean building something into the daily processes (e.g. meetings or emails). In others, where power is associated mostly with role and position, it will mean influencing the Chief Executive or selected senior people from various departments. Understand the unique aspects of your organization and how things get done. Build a network of different people in different levels and places, who will help you understand the organization from a range of perspectives. You need to learn the phrases, acronyms and way of doing things so that you can be seen as part of the organization, and not working against the tide.

10. What systems, processes and functions need to be leveraged?

This is about translating the aspiration into business as usual. It is not just about deploying HR systems like recruitment or reward (though that is part of it). It is about identifying all the other functions that need to be involved in making this a normal reality across the organization. Marketing, strategy and communications are critical partners. Too often, ego and internal politics leads to competition rather than co-operation between functions, and this is detrimental to the strategic aims of the organization and any diversity effort.

It is not for the consultant or for the OD department to own every aspect of the work. All departments need to be allowed to own and manage relevant aspects of this work. As the consultant, your role is to enable this collaboration, to inspire and guide different functions and to remove barriers so that all the functions can play their critical, professional role in making this a reality for the organization.

The more this work can be aligned to existing work, the more that it can be integrated into everyday business and the more likely it is to be sustainable. Cross-functional collaboration also leads to spread sponsorship, as many departments become invested in the success of this work.

11. What are the important power allegiances?

It is important to understand the organizational structures and where formal and informal power resides.

There may be networks within the organization that are invisible. At the top levels of the organization, there are often clans, friendships, sponsors, and allegiances. Often, those in senior levels in the organization have been there (or at least in the industry) for some time. People have usually worked with each other before, in different roles. Over time, strong relationships form. One senior leader might have a range of mentees or people who come under their umbrella of influence. As executives move jobs, sometimes the same leaders move across divisions and role as a whole team. To people new to the organization, these allegiances across management team are invisible.

It is important that any planned interventions and sponsorship involves all of the networks so that no network (clan) feels excluded as this can create an environment where one group may be motivated to sabotage the work. Different networks will have different views and access to different information. Ask questions about who these clans are, and ensure that you personally, as the consultant are never identified as a member of one of these clans. It is critical to be neutral and that you are seen to be serving the best interests of the organization.

12. What are the personal politics?

Listen for small nuances in the way people phrase words and talk of you and of the work. As the consultant, your reputation is critical. How you are discussed is important. You are the facilitator of the process, there to serve. You should not be seen to be personally symbolic of it, otherwise you run the risk of taking the project 'up' and 'down' with you as you enter and leave the limelight.

Some people may seek you out as a champion or sponsor for their own personal ambitions, others may be jealous of the prominence of a large-scale cultural project. These politics are distractions but can also be used to inform you about how the organization works, how people acquire power, and how things are done.

13. Where is there mis-alignment?

You need to pay special attention to congruence between stated values and actual behaviours in the organization. Highlight where there is a discrepancy between what is said and what is done, or between what is said and what people really believe. Are the stated values aligned with the underlying assumptions? And are the decisions and actions a reflection of the values, or is there a disconnect somewhere? And are the values, assumptions and behaviours ultimately aligned with:

- What employees want and need,
- What customers want, and
- What the overall goals of the organization are?

14. What are the internal networks and external factors that play a role?

As part of taking a systemic and networked view, you need to look closely at interconnections within and outside the organization. You need to identify what the linkages are between departments, functions, levels, geographies and how different segments in the organization are affected by (and can affect) this work. You need to be aware of how information is communicated and controlled, and where the routes of access and flow may be that help the organizational system to function smoothly – and also where blockages may be. You need to identify how communication and power flows across these real and virtual boundaries and what are the critical interfaces and points of mutual influence.

You also need to look at how this work impacts (and is impacted by) suppliers, customers, shareholders, competitors, trade bodies, industry regulators, communities and external partners. The organization doesn't exist in a bubble and it is imperative to understand it's role in society and in the communities that it serves as well as it's position in the economic and political eco-system. What are the external legal, political and economic trends that play a role and affect this work? How can the organization adapt itself to these, or affect these through its position in society?

What aspects of the national, external culture have an influence here and what is the role of the organization in affecting this? What are the different national cultures that the organization operates in and how do these align with each other and with the overall culture and values that the organization is trying to establish? Where are the points of similarity that can be leveraged and what are the important differences that will have to be managed or negotiated?

Summary

This chapter outlines some of the diagnostic work that needs to be carried out before you commence the process of culture change in any organization. The causal map outlined in the previous section provides a framework that can be used for diagnosing and understanding culture, diversity and inclusion in an organization.

It is important to take the time to immerse yourself in the organization and truly understand not only the visible elements of the culture, but the underlying assumptions and unspoken rules and ways of working through totems and symbols. This phase helps to inform the approach you take, and it also starts to builds your connection with the organization and the stakeholders within it.

To carry out a full diagnosis, you need to walk the floors and seek perspectives and stories from different areas and levels to get a full picture. You need to understand history and where the organization has come from, what shapes its current priorities, why you have been called in, what has been done already, where the key points of influence are and where the sponsorship lies. You need to get to grips with how things are done, communication routes, governance, policies and established practices that will need to be leveraged or examined in your approach. You also need to develop an awareness of key internal networks and external systemic factors that play a role. You must remain humble, neutral and curious.

Imagination

Unconscious bias has become a big buzzword across the field of Diversity & Inclusion. Most progressive organizations now seem to understand and acknowledge that as human beings, we all have innate biases, that is, that we unconsciously favour some groups (usually our own) over others, and that this leads to incorrect judgements about people and suboptimal decision-making at work. We also know that these biases are not neutral and they are formed from cultural stereotypes about particular groups (women, Muslims, Hispanics, etc.) and that although we may become aware of them (through taking the Implicit Association Test or through training), they are notoriously hard to shift. So we are at a stalemate where in organizations, there is a widespread acknowledgement of unconscious bias (and a whole industry or training and testing around it) but no clear, effective way to deal with it.

One of the main principles of our approach to Diversity & Inclusion is that we need to start with imagination. This is because we believe that imagination sits at the heart of changing mindset. It is the key that unlocks the deeply held beliefs and unconscious biases, and ultimately, imagination is the 'silver bullet' for shifting the needle on Diversity & Inclusion.

In this chapter, we describe why and how: why we believe imagination is so crucial, and how we can trigger imagination intentionally in the context of building an inclusive culture.

Why start with imagination?

It all started over a dinner conversation with a friend and esteemed colleague, John Powell. John is a Professor of Law and African American Studies at University of California, Berkeley, and an internationally recognized expert in the areas of civil rights and racism. I was talking to John about my frustration with the field of diversity and how little progress we had made in organizations after years of running various programmes and initiatives. I asked if he had any insights, or any ideas for something we might not have tried yet. His answer was one word: *propaganda*.

What did he mean? He went on to talk to me about research that had looked at the impact of the television series '24' on the US presidential race. The series made its debut in 2001 and closed in May 2009, after Barrack Obama's election. The series featured a black president, David Palmer, who was a powerful, strong and popular character. He was always cool, calm, collected and decisive – a great TV president – who had handled various attacks on the United States in a highly competent manner. He felt real and believable and human. The show was watched by millions of people who saw this black man shown in a highly positive light, playing the role of an admired and strong president. This imagery was powerful enough to perhaps shift people's unconscious thinking and influence the real possibility of a black president being elected. The *New York Times* in January 2009 ran an article titled 'How the Movies Made a President'. It looked at how positive black archetypes in movies and TV prepared the ground for Obama. Of course the link is not so simple or straightforward and of course Obama's election was very much down to his own capability, but there has been a lot of research and commentary about how the media and representation of white and black people can change the way people think about race and the associations people make.

Strong, recurring, positive images of a black president in the media created the possibility of a black president in reality by sowing the cognitive seeds. More people watch prime time television than watch the political shows and the news. The entertainment media is more dramatic and places a strong impression upon the mind. It shapes our unconscious attitudes, which then guide our behaviour.

John's advice got us thinking about the impact of media on imagination and we wanted to know more about how this plays out in our brains.

We read the work of American Psychiatrist and Neuroscientist, Jeffery Schwartz, who talked about how learnt behaviours like obsessive-compulsive disorder (OCD) can be 'cured' through the treatment of imagination. In 2012, Schwartz spoke at a United Nations conference, about his work with actor Leonardo DiCaprio, who played Howard Hughes, a man suffering from OCD, in the film *The Aviator*. Schwartz explained that sometimes actors get so involved in the role that it can actually change their personality and brain chemistry. He reported that after learning about OCD for the role that he played in the film, DiCaprio actually developed OCD himself and had to be treated for three months to remove the symptoms.

Behavioural psychologists suggest that compulsive behaviours are developed and maintained through mental conditioning – they are learnt behaviours, which help an individual deal with anxiety or discomfort associated with obsessions. Cognitive psychologists believe OCD is rooted in faulty or dysfunctional beliefs, which lead to maladaptive, compulsive behaviours, which are learnt over time. Using the imagination, these behaviours can be unlearnt and neural pathways can be 'rewired'. If this is the case, then why can't unconscious bias or prejudice (which is also a learnt and faulty belief) be 'treated' in the same way: using imagination?

We know that imagination creates new possibilities for us. If we have a good example in front of us, of a strong and effective black US president (even a fictitious one on TV), it becomes a not-too-unrealistic possibility in the real world. In the earlier section, we described some studies that showed that if we imagine ourselves in a black person's shoes (or play a video game as a black avatar) even for a few minutes, we come out having a higher level of empathy with black people.[1] If we look at images of positive black role models just before we take the IAT test, we score much lower on anti-black bias.[2] If we make ourselves imagine having a pleasant and positive interaction with an elderly person, or a Muslim person (even for only two minutes and even if we know it is a figment of our imagination), we come out having more positive feelings for these groups.[3] The imagination is powerful, it's where our beliefs originate and it is what ignites behaviour.

High-profile organizations have the power to shift public perception and change stereotypes through role modelling.

I spoke with some colleagues in India about female representation in senior roles in various industries. To my surprise, they said that most of the highly qualified females, especially business school graduates, are being 'snapped up' by financial services organizations these days (leaving few for other industries) because finance is seen as a desirable area of work for women. I found this strange because banking and finance is seen as a traditionally male-dominated industry in most of the Western world. Yet in India, the perception seemed to be that banking is one of the few areas where women can 'really progress'. How do they draw this conclusion? They tell me it's because the Chief Executive of ICICI, a major Indian financial services organization, is a woman, as is the Group General Manager and Country Head of HSBC India. Just a couple of such high profile senior appointments have managed to completely shift public perception of what is normal and possible for women, leading to a surge of qualified women now wanting to enter banking in India.

It seems obvious now, that if we want to change a culture, we have to work on behaviour as well as beliefs. It is ineffective to try and force people to do things differently just through rules and policies and procedures, if they subconsciously hold on to the same old ways of thinking. We have to tackle the 'belief' level of Diversity & Inclusion. We have to take on the challenge of shifting unconscious biases and open up new ways of thinking about each other. We have to move mind-sets. And in order to do this, we have to begin with imagination.

As we write this book, a new series is on American screens called *Madam Secretary*. It shows a white blond woman who is thrust into the role of Secretary of State in the White House. As we count down to the next US presidential election in 2016, we will leave you to speculate on what impact it might have on the minds and ideas of people watching. (The female lead in this show looks remarkably like Hilary Clinton.)

How do you trigger imagination?

Seeing is believing. And believing is behaving. What we see around us creates our beliefs and ideas of what is real or possible, and what is normal and good and desirable. Our beliefs then impact how we behave, how we see ourselves and others and what expectations we have, and thus they *create* reality. This is why it is so crucial to look at the beliefs we hold, before we can start to change anything else. We are limited by our beliefs and by the ideas and stereotypes that we hold. Until we can imagine something new as a real possibility, it can never happen.

So how do we create new possibilities in our minds? We go back to the advice from John Powell: '*propaganda*'.

Propaganda is intentional communication that has been traditionally used to influence individuals and society as a whole. Humans have always used it since the earliest tools of communication have begun. It links with the idea of priming, discussed in Chapter 6. Priming is a memory effect in which exposure to certain stimulus impacts how we respond to another stimulus after that.

In the UK, in the week preceding Armistice Day, the British Broadcasting Corporation (BBC) ran a few stories of individual soldiers and spies who had made a significant difference in the wars. One big story was about a Sikh man and another, about a Muslim man, both of whom made personal sacrifices and fought bravely in the war to defend the nation. The timing of these stories appearing in the BBC was not a coincidence; it was at the time of the year when national pride and patriotism is at its height but also a time when 'Britishness' is brought into the spotlight. Stories like these help to build up the timely narrative about Britishness being linked with multiculturalism, that both the Sikh and the Muslim man are British and have fought for their country.

Stories like this which appear in the media in such a timely way may be intentionally (politically) generated or they may have naturally arisen in the context of current affairs. Either way, they hold power in shaping the ideas and emotions of the public. These stories, for example, remind us, at a key moment in our history, that 'they' are one of 'us'. Reading the story about the Sikh and the Muslim soldier helps to 're-set' our thinking about these groups as we go out into the world. It primes us to respond in a (hopefully) more tolerant, empathic and respectful way.

Positive Intentional Communication

Organizations already use propaganda. Considerable funds and time are spent on designing advertisements that are aimed at convincing consumers to buy products or make positive associations with their brands. A sophisticated range of multimedia channels are used to impact public opinion and emotion in this way. Organizations thus already know what it takes to influence humans in the pursuit of profit.

To use the same principles internally means to use media and communication to convey the new and positive associations we want to create amongst our employees. It means tactically designing positive communication campaigns across the organization that leverages images and language that have the desired impact.

The word 'propaganda' can have negative connotations, and it is sometimes viewed as a form of coercion, or control with a typically negative end. In this context, the end is not negative, it is carefully designed to be positive, aspirational and targeted to the betterment of the organization as a whole. If the word 'propaganda' feels negative to you, consider an alternative: 'Positive Intentional Communication'.

The purpose is to show positive images of non-stereotypical leaders and role models. It is about intentionally and carefully countering some of the biases that we know are prevalent by highlighting images that slowly, over time shake the old, erroneous associations that we hold to allow space for new ways of thinking about ourselves and our groups.

In partnership with internal communications and marketing teams, a wide range of media can be used to build a strong and consistent campaign over time. The purpose of the work is to send messages to define what the organization is all about, to articulate the collective aspiration, to define the internal and external brand and align messages of equality, inclusion and tolerance of difference with the same messages and images that define the brand of the company.

At one organization, we ran a campaign to counter stereotypes and create new ideas of what leadership can look like. As part of this, we had an image of a smart and competent Mergers & Acquisitions lawyer, with three tag lines underneath the image:

M&A Lawyer with a 100% case win ratio

Educated from a top university

Gay

When we ran this campaign, there had been hesitation about explicitly putting an image of a gay person up. There was hesitation about calling out an LBGT agenda on the corporate website due to the global nature of the organization and the sensitivities in some cultures. There were concerns about whether some employees would find even the word 'gay' prominently displayed inappropriate.

In the end, the board decided to run it. The image, among others, appeared globally on screen savers and posters. After a few weeks (at the global headquarters), we started to get messages and emails, from across the company. People said things like: 'I have worked in the company for fifteen years and I have just come out to my team, thank you.' The impact of the image was to make being gay normal and not taboo in this company. In the weeks and months after, membership of the LGBT affinity group swelled. An invisible but significant segment of the workforce had been given the message that they were accepted and valued and part of the Brand.

Is propaganda ethical?

The word propaganda often bears negative connotations because it is seen to be a form of manipulation of peoples' thoughts and opinions.

In reality, however, propaganda or any media cannot really create new ideas; it always builds on ideas that already exist in some shape or form in peoples' minds already. So, for example, if an ad for a perfume depicts a handsome, young man without a shirt on, surrounded by attractive women, what it's trying to tell us is that buying this perfume will make me sexually attractive like him. It is a manipulation of our thoughts because it is leading us to make a mental association between the perfume and sexuality or attractiveness – but it has not created the idea of sexual attraction or defined it for us. It has used the concept that already exists in our minds. It has just carefully linked that concept with the product it is trying to sell, and this is where the line is hazy.

There is potential for propaganda to be used in different ways and to different ends.

Organizations already use propaganda in their advertising and marketing to help them sell products and create a desirable brand image and identity. Politicians use propaganda to help project a particular image about themselves or their political parties or to bring their agendas to the table. Governments use propaganda to create ideologies and influence the way people think about current affairs and issues and to create cultural discourses and ways of thinking. Propaganda is used through the media to counter potentially disruptive thinking: for example, in the United States, after the terrorist attacks of 9/11, there were a series of advertisements, which showed a rolling amorphous face that changed race and gender. Each new face said the words 'I'm an American'. The adverts were a sponsored attempt by the government to show that American citizens came in variety of races. It was designed to limit a potential reaction of racial attacks on Muslims, Sikhs and others who might be seen as non-American and to bring unity to the nation at a time of national crisis.

Propaganda is also used positively by government to change behaviour, for example ad campaigns to help people stop smoking or drive slower, or to create greater community cohesion and harmony.

We have to be clear in our context that what we mean by propaganda is not to deviously manipulate people's minds to suit our own selfish needs or to help the organization sell its products or make money. In this context, the term refers to using media and communication to counter prevailing stereotypes and prejudice, instil beliefs that are positive, fair and rational, and create an environment, which is equal and inclusive. We refer to it as positive intentional communication.

The deliberate shaping of culture can be done in a transparent way and with integrity. This is not a covert government action seeking to influence its citizens to support military or domestic agendas. This is the organization intentionally executing on what it has promised to do in its values statements, it's commitment to creating an inclusive culture. It is saying that if you join us, you will need to commit to particular behaviours and viewpoints.

Employees should not be surprised by any of the images or stories, instead they should recognize and welcome that the organization is delivering on its promise. In our experience, employees welcome this, regardless of background as it creates an environment where all, including the majority are treated with respect.

Appreciative Inquiry and storytelling

Alongside the large-scale communications campaign, it is also necessary to spark dialogue in the organization at a more local level. There are two effective methods to do this, which go hand in hand with each other: Appreciative Inquiry (AI) and storytelling. These two, in tandem, start conversations across the organization which help to articulate and refine the collective aspiration of the organization and raise awareness and excitement about the vision.

The role of storytelling

On 15 December 2014, the BBC reported:

As a gunman holds people hostage in a cafe in Sydney, thousands of messages of support have been posted online for Muslims in Australia who are afraid of an Islamophobic backlash. The spark was this post on Facebook by Rachael Jacobs, who said she'd seen a woman she presumed was Muslim silently removing her hijab while sitting next to her on the train: 'I ran after her at the train station. I said "put it back on. I'll walk with u." She started to cry and hugged me for about a minute – then walked off alone'.

- What impact does this story have on you?
- What's it like, would you say, to be Muslim and living in Sydney?
- What do you conclude about 'What people are like' in Sydney, about how Muslims are treated there?

Whether consciously or subconsciously, stories like this in the news and media affect our ideas and thought processes: they create cultural narratives. In particular, stories that evoke emotion, like 'I'll walk with you' bring about powerful feelings and energy around an issue – even more so than an ad or a change in the law might be able to do. When we make a connection, especially an emotional one, with someone in a story like this, our empathy and our passion is evoked. We start to care, we understand the issue more acutely, and we want to take part in creating a solution. No wonder thousands of people re-tweeted 'I'll walk with you' (offering to meet Muslims on public transport and accompany them on their journeys), and it became a spontaneous viral campaign.

Storytelling is one of the oldest ways in which cultures were created and maintained, well before the internet or print media. Stories articulate ideas and create discourses. Telling culturally significant stories is a way of expressing what 'we are about' as stories highlight characteristics of people or of a group, or it can illustrate principles, morals and values.

In organizations, there is an opportunity to leverage this age-old method for shaping human opinion and culture through the positive use of storytelling. Organizational stories can be used to articulate values and propagate ideas around inclusion, and what it means. In this way, stories form part of propaganda as much as advertising, posters, imagery and logos. In some ways, stories – because they are 'real' – can be even more powerful than other communications, and they can work on the subconscious level of human understanding.

Storytelling is how we humans create, share and interpret experiences. Stories can bridge cultural, linguistic and philosophical divides across a multiple of demographics. Storytelling can be used as a method to teach ethics, values, and cultural norms and differences and is applicable across ages. Stories pass on knowledge in a social context and are how any human organization thrives and re-creates their culture one conversation at a time. They are a powerful tool that taps into how we naturally think and learn.

Once I was working on a project to create a new a new aspect of culture; I talked to one of the senior officers in the company and asked for an example of the type of culture that we were looking to become. He told me a story about how this behaviour came alive in his previous company (a well-known fizzy drinks brand). The brand had power (because it is a household name) and thus the story had power because it was associated to the brand and also to the fact that the senior officer himself had power in the organization. I then deliberately shared the story widely at different levels in the organization. Six months later, I was at a dinner when I was talking to a colleague about the work, and she turned to me and said, 'do you know what (insert fizzy drinks brand) do every day?' She had heard the story in a speech at a regional sales meeting. The story had come back to me. It was alive in the culture, and it was slowly working to create a particular narrative in the organization.

Think carefully about where you may hear stories in the organization, and how you can go about finding stories from different perspectives and places. Consider what messages lie behind these stories, which ones you might wish to circulate to build or describe inclusion, and how you would go about doing this.

The stories that start the work and the stories that are circulated at the end are different. At the beginning of the process there are stories to inspire and this means that they are usually from the past. There are stories about dreams that are shared from sponsors. In the middle there are stories about how things are starting to be different, examples of how this work is being taken forward with passion, that give people permission to be different themselves. Towards the later stages of the evolution, there are stories of small victories, of how the positive difference is impacting people, profits, winning business differently, making customers delighted and showing how it was all worth it. As the consultant, you are the 'keeper of stories'. Listen out for what people are talking about across the organization. Look for themes and share the stories.

Appreciative Inquiry (AI)

The process of Appreciative Inquiry (AI) was developed by David Cooperrider in the late 1980s at Case Western University (USA), but it is now widely used in various settings all over the world.

> It is a method for organizational change that is based on a working with groups of people to talk about, identify and articulate the positive aspects of culture and describe the collective hopes. It is defined in different ways, for example: '*Appreciative Inquiry is the co-operative co-evolutionary search for the best in people, their organizations and the world around them.*'[4]

AI was developed as a counter-point to the traditional approaches of problem-solving.[5] Rather than focusing on what is wrong and what needs repair, AI focuses on the desired outcome – where we want to be. It works by posing the 'unconditional positive question' to large numbers of people to evoke collective imagination, hope and innovation. It is a systemic and participatory approach to Organizational Development that is based on the principles of constructionism that is, that reality is subjective and created by our personal perspectives and narratives. So stories play a key role here in shaping how we see things.

There are four phases of AI:[6]

- Discovery (Appreciating and identifying the best aspects of where we are)
- Dream (Envisioning an ideal future state)
- Design (Co-constructing ways to build this into everyday life)
- Destiny (Sustaining the momentum)

> Example:
>
> *The 'Dream Activity' in relation to inclusion*
>
> Close your eyes, and imagine that you are five years from today. Imagine that everything that you have ever hoped for is true in your place of work. You can

truly say, without reservation, that this is an inclusive organization that is free from prejudice and everyone has the same opportunities.

What does it feel like to work in this new organization?

How do people treat one another?

What is the leadership like?

How do employees behave?

How do our customers perceive us?

How do our business partners feel about us?

One of the challenges in introducing the use of Appreciative Inquiry is that many organizations have an established problem solving methodology, e.g. fact-based gap analysis such as Six Sigma or Lean. They are well-trained to ask 'What problem are we solving for here?'. Care should be taken to explain why positive images are important here and what the benefits are to taking a more aspirational rather than a problem-focused approach.

The power of AI is that it creates energy amongst participants. Rather than feeling like you are working at resolving something negative, it creates the sense that you are collectively working at creating something positive. It instils hope and positivity because you are working towards and not away from something. The dreams we share as a team are powerful and positive. We can as organizations articulate a future as we want it to be, feel like, etc. As we talk about our collective dreams, we are in fact setting the stage for our imagination to be allowed to guide us in creating a new future.

By tapping into individual and collective imagination, AI helps to generate positive and powerful stories in line with an aspirational future. In AI, employees talk about personal and shared experiences and hopes, in the context of what we want to focus on (a more inclusive environment) and collectively imagine and describe what an idea future state would look like for the organization.

AI is a very effective way to invigorate the discussion about culture. It can be directed to focus on any aspect. For example, to get people to start thinking about inclusion, you openly ask individuals to tell stories about a time in their life where they had really felt included, and what that was like. This can focus on the current workplace, previous jobs, or wider life. The important thing is that rather than just telling people to be inclusive, you are inspiring them to think about the positive aspects of inclusion and get in touch with the real feeling or experience as one that is aspirational.

The result is that you collect stories and themes that are based on peoples' real experiences. These themes can then be shared and used to define what inclusion means here, what is aspirational about it and inspire others through story-sharing.

In addition, the process in itself can be motivational. The act of telling the stories, in what is essentially a style of positive focus group, being heard by others, can make people feel more positive about the themes they are talking about. They share, reflect, give feedback and work off mutual energy to create a 'buzz' around the topic. People who took part tell others about the experience, and they recount the stories they told and heard and the word spreads, creating energy along the way. The process of talking about positive culture change, in itself becomes a method for positive culture change. This can then be supplemented by the formal process of collating stories by theme and linking them to corporate language or interventions.

In the final phases of the work, the team can look at what dreams and stories emerge, and based on this they can:

- Co-construct a future vision for the organization
- Articulate the properties of the desired culture/ what 'good' looks like
- Identify what changes are most likely to help achieve a culture of inclusion
- Design appropriate interventions, strategies, processes and campaigns

Through the stories that come up in this process, we demonstrate that we already have the ability and the inclination to act in the way that we hope for. The targeted behaviour/mindset is already in us, and we already know what 'good' looks like.

The next task is to consider the scale of what is most urgent, what links with the work can create a 'quick win' for the organization and then make choices about what to fund and sponsor immediately.

In one organization, a local regional team had developed an online 'storyboard' to share peoples' personal examples about how the organization has respected diversity. We took this idea and made it global. In the Middle East, a story was written into an open and on-line employee forum. A mid-level employee said that at birth he had been born with significant physical illness. He described how he had not been able to attend school but had been home schooled. He had found it difficult to find work. The organization had offered him a junior entry-level clerical job and given him training. He had worked hard and over the years, he had been promoted. At every step of the way, he had been given the tools and the support he required to enable him to perform his work. Office spaces and entrances had been amended. He was now a manager, and in his note, he thanked the company emotionally for their support of his difference.

The story went viral globally around the company with employees writing in from all over the world thanking him for sharing his experience, and wishing him well. His individual experience sparked a global feeling across the organization of empathy, warmth, inspiration and pride, more so than any employee communications campaign could ever have done.

There are often outstanding local solutions and inspiring personal stories that are not known to the whole organization or to the global corporate teams. The invitation to celebrate such local achievements, and to creatively articulate what inclusion means in a real sense, releases energy and gives pride and inspiration to continue the work.

Summary

Any change in a person or in a society begins with imagination – the ability to see things differently, to envision a new possibility. If we cannot imagine things being different, the reality will never be. This is one of the fundamental ideas in this book – that, in order to shift our personal and our cultural biases and move past our 'stuckness' in Diversity & Inclusion, we must intentionally create a programme whereby we seek to trigger peoples' imaginations and offer hope for a new way of thinking.

In organizations, we have the opportunity and the responsibility to influence and spread ideas about equality, tolerance and inclusion. We can use propaganda, storytelling and Appreciative Inquiry in a systematic, ethical and positive way to spread positive cultural narratives about inclusion.

1   Peck, T. C., Seinfeld, S., Aglioti, S. M., & Slater, M. (2013). Putting yourself in the skin of a black avatar reduces implicit racial bias. *Consciousness and Cognition, 22*(3), 779–787.

2   Dasgupta, N. & Greenwald, A. G. (2001). On the malleability of automatic attitudes: Combating automatic prejudice with images of admired and disliked individuals. *Journal of Personality and Social Psychology, 81*(5), 800.

3   Turner, R. N., & Crisp, R. J. (2010). Imagining intergroup contact reduces implicit prejudice. *British Journal of Social Psychology, 49*(1), 129–114.

4   Cooperrider, D., Whitney, D. D., & Stavros, J. M. (2008). *The appreciative inquiry handbook: For leaders of change.* Berrett-Koehler Publishers. USA.

5   Cooperrider, D. L. & Srivastva, S. (1987). Appreciative Inquiry in organizational life. In Woodman, R. W. & Pasmore, W.A. (eds) *Research in Organizational Change and Development*, Vol. 1 (129–169). Stamford, CT: JAI Press.

6   Cooperrider, D., Whitney, D. D., & Stavros, J. M. (2008). *The appreciative inquiry handbook: For leaders of change.* Berrett-Koehler Publishers. USA.

Chapter 16
Leadership and behaviour

Chapter Outline

The study and development of 'leadership' is a central aspect of HR and OD work in organizations. A lot of emphasis is put on the capability and selection of leaders because they are seen to be core to how well an organization performs. Leaders set the tone for others; they make the big decisions that affect everyone and have the most control over the direction and destiny of the organization. Leadership and behaviour are naturally linked because leaders decide what behaviours are acceptable or desirable, and they role model these behaviours for the rest of the organization.

In the area of Diversity, work on 'leadership' usually takes the approach of training women or minorities on how to be better leaders or how to act in the corporate world through targeted coaching. The focus is on *who* is in leadership (e.g. percentage of women or minority ethnic employees at senior role levels) rather than understanding what *kind of leadership* is needed to create an inclusive culture.

In this chapter, we want to challenge some of the prevailing views about leadership and recommend a new way of looking at leadership that is more compatible with the context we operate in today and more aligned with the work of creating culture change. We also want to describe the qualities that are crucial in leadership in order to facilitate a transition to a more inclusive and diverse culture and suggest ways in which behaviour can be changed at an organizational level through leadership and role modelling.

The top-down model

Changing culture implies changing peoples' everyday, normal behaviours – creating new *ways* of how people act with each other at work. In most large organizations, behaviour has traditionally been managed in a top-down fashion. Typically, the senior management team decides what behaviours are allowed or not allowed (this may be influenced by external factors like legislation or competition), and then HR creates a policy around it, and it is enforced through the use of reward (e.g. pay, bonuses, promotion, recognition) or punishment (e.g. disciplinary, warnings, dismissals or withholding reward). This approach is based on motivating people through the use of fear and threat, and it is based on a narrow, behaviourist view of human nature.

Even in more complex culture change initiatives where other means of motivating and changing people are considered (e.g. values led behaviour or authentic leadership), the assumption tends to be that it must occur at the top first and then trickle down to the bottom. More often than not, the 'top 100' or the 'top team' goes through the intervention or training programme before the rest of the employee population, and there is a heavy reliance on leaders and managers to enforce desired behaviours among employees.

Conventional leadership development programmes typically focus on the most senior teams. Few focus on what is referred to as 'middle management'. They are called middles because of where they sit in a typical hierarchical pyramid. They watch the top of the organization swirl and change above them while they lead the rest of the organization at a day to day level. They are often neglected and yet they are the critical definers of any organizational change because of their direct influence on the majority of employees.

There is no doubt that leaders and managers play an important role. They have direct influence on employee behaviour and can help to sustain new ways of behaving, not just through enforcement, but also through encouragement, engagement, recognition and role modelling.

However, rather than thinking about only 'top' of the pyramid, or even thinking in levels at all, it may be more useful to think about the whole *system of leadership*. This means understanding and charting the roles of the different groups and types of leaders in the organization – those at the top, or the middle, and those that can emerge in different places at different levels as the need arises.

In *The Tipping Point* (2000), Malcolm Gladwell shows that there is usually a group (called 'early adopters') in every organization or society, who are more open to new ideas and are the first to take them on and start new trends. They are easier to work with, will help iron out early implementation blocks to any initiative and provide an energy that is contagious to the rest of the organization. They are 'leaders' in their own way, because they carry the ability to create followership and contagion. In order to kick start any change effort, it is worth identifying this group – and this is not always those who are most senior.

New generations entering the workforce learn in new ways and have different expectations from their employer. When seeking advice or new knowledge, they may look to each other and they look outside the organization as much as they look upwards to their managers or others inside their organization. Social media becomes the platform for learning, dialogue and culture-creation. Increasingly, the boundaries of the office as a place of work, the structural hierarchy, job titles and even the organization as such, are blurred, as the world is getting more fluid and more connected.

The top-down model alone is insufficient in this context. There is a new way of thinking about leadership that will be far more helpful in creating sustainable behaviour change in today's organizations.

A non-hierarchical alternative

The word leadership generally implies a group of people at the top – often the board or the top-level managers. Even in wider society, leadership often implies particular people who are in power. Yet the concept of leadership can also be thought of as a quality or as a process, and it doesn't always have to be situated in a person, there can be groups who lead. We draw on some emergent and exciting ideas of leadership discussed by Simon Western.[1]

Western introduces us to the concept of 'eco-leadership', which is a much more relevant conceptualization of leadership in the context of creating sustainable change in today's complex organizations. Traditional hierarchical models of leadership do not account for the networked world we live in, and they don't allow space for emergence in cultural change. *Eco Leadership* focuses on creating connections and spaces for leadership to emerge and thrive throughout the organization wherever it is necessary not just at the top. It accesses talent in the moment and relies on wisdom and collective intelligence to deal with increasing organizational and societal complexity.

When we talk about *leadership development*, then, rather than thinking about training the few people at the top of an organization in a set of narrow skills, we should consider ways in which we can create a culture that enables the emergence of inclusive leadership throughout the organization. We need to understand what the nature of such leadership needs to be, what qualities we need in our leaders everywhere and how to foster this across the organization.

What qualities do we need in leaders?

Self-awareness

Self-insight is probably the most important quality in the context of culture change and diversity. Leaders need to have the curiosity and openness to understand their own biases as well as the humility to know when to listen and seek counsel. They must be aware of their own place, position and power (in society and in the organization) and be able to confront their own biases and prejudice as well as organizational limitations with openness.

Equanimity

Change can be difficult, even when it is positive, and there is always risk of backlash and challenge. Leaders need to be able to regulate their own emotional response and maintain a state of equanimity through the challenge of leading others through change. This is important particularly in this context where the work can bring up issues that are personal or linked with strong aspects of one's identity.

Adaptability

One popular model of leadership used in OD is 'Situational Leadership'.[2] The essence of the model is that the most effective leaders do not just follow one uniform method, but they also adapt their style to meet the needs of those who they lead. This means having the ability to modify how directive or how supportive you are based on what is needed in a particular situation. This idea of adaptability is key to the principle of inclusion.

Humility

Situational leadership is often connected to the concept of 'servant leadership',[3] where the purpose of leadership is seen primarily to serve others within the organization, with humility and concern for others being key principles, rather than ego. Rather than accumulating power, the role of the leader is to share power and enable others to do well. Again, this is key to inclusion because the leader serves to bring out the best in others, and this requires flexibility as well as an understanding of diverse needs. We will not expand on these two concepts here but highly recommend them as additional reading.

Critical analytic thinking

Critical analytic thinking includes the ability to look at the big picture (beyond the current situation), understand wider contextual factors, make links and consider different viewpoints. Empathy and imagination both rely on the ability to see things abstractly from another perspective – in other words, to *transcend* the immediate reality. This mental ability also sits at the heart of transcultural competence, that is, having the skill to be able to incorporate multiple cultural and philosophical perspectives to resolve problems and pursue a richer truth.

Meta-thinking

Another key skill related to critical thinking is *metacognition* – to think *about thinking*. Metacognition means being able to understand one's own cognitive process and emotional state with detachment and objectivity. It is to know not just *what* decisions to make but also being aware of *how* you make decisions. It is being aware of what you personally tend to prioritize and give importance to and what you value. It is knowing when to think fast and use your gut and when you need to slow down and deliberate. It knowing when and how to engage both 'fast' and 'slow' thinking and being able to reflect on what factors influence this. This ability starts to bring some of our unconscious decision-making processes into our conscious awareness so we can address when they are not optimal or inclusive.

Empathy

In order to be intrinsically motivated by the aims of this work, empathy is key. Empathy is the ability to look at things from another person's perspective, to be able to imagine being in someone else's shoes. This implies:

- the capacity to abstract from one's own position to conceptualize how a certain policy or practice might affect someone from a different background
- an appreciation of the negative impact of bias and discrimination on the organization and society as a whole (even when it is not one's own group being discriminated against)

The core group of the organization (usually the senior-most and a few select others) tend to hold much of the power and influence. Yet, as people gain more power, they tend to show a reduction in their level of empathy with those who have less power. This is the irony of trying to create such a cultural change – those who are most able to change things have the least motivation to do so, because they are already in positions where they have nothing materially to gain (or so it may seem). Due to the nature of their work and the time constraints they are often under, their day-to-day contact often becomes limited to those at the same level as them (and usually these are people from similar backgrounds in society). As a result, their perspective becomes limited and they lose touch with the diverse needs and concerns of the majority of the organization. This is evident in most employee surveys, where the scores of the senior-most executives are generally significantly different from the rest of the organization. Without a realistic perspective of another's position, one cannot have empathy. For successful change, it is necessary to intentionally help senior-most executives to gain the perspective and empathy needed to invest in this work.

Leadership development and behaviour change

So, how do we foster these qualities in our leaders throughout the organization and enable large-scale behaviour change?

Bridging the empathy gap

For the senior team, the core group, to send the message in a clear and genuine way to the rest of the organization, they must believe it themselves. They must be personally committed to the aims; for this, empathy and passion is key. Senior executives are often too removed from everyday functioning of the organization or the perspectives of those who are far below them on the ladder. There are tactical ways to help bridge this gap. The following list is not exhaustive but illustrative of the obvious and simple things that can be done:

Skip level lunch

In hierarchical organizations, you often see symbols which separate senior executives from everyone else such as an executive dining room or a special lift to the executive floor. These physical and symbolic separators create a sense of 'specialness' among the senior-most but they also create a barrier.

The 'skip level lunch' is an intervention that attempts to remove such a barrier. Executives of different levels meet over lunch or dinner in an open and less formal setting. Typically senior-most leaders eat with those who are two levels below them. Food is something that is common to all humans, regardless of gender, race, class, age or role level. The shared experience of having a meal together creates a context where employees can talk more freely about their experiences and perceptions rather than feeling like they have to conform to role-level expectations and protocol.

Reverse mentoring

In reverse mentoring, a one-to-one relationship is set up between a senior executive and a more junior employee, where the junior employee is tasked with being a 'mentor' for the senior executive. The rationale is that regardless of level, an employee who represents a different background or generation or perspective can help to widen the thinking of the executive and help them gain a new perspective. For reverse mentoring to work to its full potential, leaders need to be open and humble about their own position. They need to acknowledge that there may be something they can learn from those who are more junior than them, and see this as a valuable interaction, otherwise it can come across as a 'fad' that is not taken seriously. For employees who become reverse mentors, this can be a very empowering experience, where they feel listened to and valued for their personal perspective. Through their direct connection with leadership, they feel truly part of the organization and often become champions of the change that you intend to drive.

We set up a reverse mentoring programme in a large, global organization, where (like many organizations), senior managers were predominantly white, upper middle-class straight men with a private education. There were no openly gay members of staff at a senior level. We paired one senior executive with an openly gay male employee, who was from a different race and considerably younger. They met frequently. When the executive encountered an issue in their daily work that they wanted another perspective on, they would call their 'mentor', and ask for their view on the issue. At the end of the first year, the senior executive decided that for the first time, the company should have a float in the annual Pride parade in the city. The executive marched in the parade next to the float. This had been relatively unthinkable for the company previously and represented a big leap forward in creating a culture that was inclusive on the basis of sexual orientation.

Focus on person not just task

Typically, we train managers to focus on task, that is, the work-related goals of each team member. While we know that people-management is an equally (if not more) important aspect of management, this is not usually rewarded or enforced enough through formal organizational process, which tends to focus on targets, sales, performance management, absenteeism, and so on.

If we give leaders and managers the time and space to focus not only on task but also on people, we can help them to understand the people in their teams better. We should encourage them to make personal connections, to gain new perspectives and to learn from members of their team. They need to ask: Who are the *people* in my team (not just the roles)? What will be important to them in the year ahead? Why have they chosen to work in this organization? What do they want in their lives? What are their priorities and how does inclusion affect them?

A day in the life

Consider asking leaders to spend time where their employees spend time, as part of an induction to a new type of leadership. Try shopping in a different place in town to see where workers in the team might shop. Understand what their typical day at work is like and the financial (and other) choices that they make daily for their family.

Curiosity is key here. Encourage those in management roles to show an interest in difference not to ignore it. Give leaders the opportunity to explore what lies beyond their personal perspectives and in-groups. This is an intentional attempt to widen what they see as 'my group' and increase empathy and understanding of other perspectives.

In setting such activity up, it is important to also be transparent about what we are trying to do. It should not be put forward as a 'treatment' of bias or as a reparative action. It should be posited as a positive choice and an opportunity to pursue new awareness and insight.

Message from the top

In almost all the work we have done on organizational change, one key factor always emerges, and this is the importance of vision and commitment from the top. Employees are often sceptical of diversity statements because they are seen to be 'ticking the box' or just marketing, and not really form a core part of the company's operation that is taken seriously or invested in.

If inclusion is to be taken seriously and incorporated into everyday work, then it needs to be seen to be one of the key operating principles. This means not just including a diversity statement in the company mission statement, but actually sending a strong, loud and clear message to all employees that the organization is serious about this through actions not just words.

Address bias in an honest, open way

De-criminalize bias

Each of us has our own implicit biases. The problem is when we try to ignore, hide or deny our biases instead of confronting and addressing them. Suppression or denial doesn't make bias go away, it may just hide it from obvious view and make it even more ingrained. In order to move past the current stagnation within Diversity and Inclusion, we have to start with *de-criminalizing* bias. Often, the fear of being branded a racist or a sexist or saying something that is not politically correct can be the biggest obstacle for open conversations about diversity. Once this fear is taken away, we can start to have more authentic, meaningful and helpful conversations about diversity.

Encourage self-reflection

We should take a curious rather than a defensive stance. We should start to explore where our biases come from, what impact they may be having and how we become more aware and mindful of them in our daily decision-making. Senior-most leaders must start with themselves so that the rest of the organization can feel safe in doing the same without fear of reprisal.

Tools like the Implicit Associations Test (IAT) offer a concrete way to build self-awareness about one's own biases and a practical starting point for conversations about prejudice and inclusion at a larger scale. These should be used in a way that encourages self-learning and openness, and should not be seen to be a 'test' or a punitive measure.

Seek to shift bias and challenge stereotypes

Awareness itself doesn't get rid of bias. This is where much of the 'unconscious bias training' in organizations gets stuck. We also need to really make an effort to understand where the biases come from and think of creative ways in which we can reduce their impact. We need to identify what stereotypes we hold and what associations we make as well as understand the limitations of the evidence and personal experience we draw on when doing so. We need to treat our biases as 'irrational, unhelpful beliefs' (to use a phrase from cognitive behavioural therapy) and seek to adjust them by being mindful of their impact on our everyday thoughts, decisions and actions.

The task is to expand our minds in two ways:

1. *By having new experiences to counter our stereotypes and widen our range of evidence*
   For example sitting next to someone new, or from a different background, expanding our circle of friends, talking to someone who has a different perspective, breaking out of our comfort zone and in-groups to educate ourselves on other ways of thinking and perceiving the world
2. *By becoming more attuned to our cognitive processes*
   For example being mindful of our thoughts and feelings, reflecting critically on how we make decisions, stopping to check whether we are reacting with our gut (limbic system) or thinking rationally

Once we know our biases, we can take active steps to expose ourselves to new situations and information that challenges them. We can actively seek out opportunities to change how we think, contributing to a powerful process of personal and organizational change.

Diversity training

There is a wide range of 'diversity training' available today. At the minimum, they are not only aimed at preventing equal rights violations at work and employer liability by making employees aware of laws and policies but also used as a vehicle for promoting cultural awareness, inclusion and effective team-working.

It is important to understand what the primary goal of the training is: is it basically driven by a need to avoid non-compliance with legislation? Or is it trying to create positive cultural change? How is the success of the training measured: numbers attended, attendee satisfaction or changes in behaviour? And how soon after the training is the impact expected?

The best training programmes are the ones that take the widest possible view of diversity and address the nuanced ways in which all kinds of perceived differences impact our thinking and behaviour. They address multiple layers of personal identity and focus not only on big, visible behaviours but also raise awareness of small, non-verbal cues that can create micro-inequities. They also provide some personal guidance on how to address and shift bias using the steps outlined earlier.

There is also an additional value in such training programmes (which is not always leveraged), and that is the opportunity that they provide for open and honest discussion. Often, diversity training programmes focus on educating employees about legislation or rules, and they create a fear of non-compliance. Instead, these sessions, if conducted appropriately, can be used as a non-judgemental platform where employees can express their thoughts, feelings, fears and hopes. This type of platform is not often available at the workplace. It provides the opportunity for people to come together to discuss aspirational ways in which *difference* can be turned into a strength, and how personal self-awareness can enhance one's life experience, to create positive outcomes individually, organizationally and socially.

Pay attention to *how* people behave, not just *what* they do

In order to examine culture, we need to look at how we do everything with a critical eye. This means putting a spotlight not only on what is being done in the organization but also how it is done. This is not just the 'big tasks' such as production or recruitment, but also the little, everyday tasks, for example, how and where and when do we run meetings? How are decisions made, by whom, and what message does this send out about the culture? This is discussed in more detail in Chapter 17.

Where traditional ways of working are highlighted as being problematic, exclusionary or potentially stagnating, we need to be brave in trying new methods. For example, make a point of paying attention to those who don't speak as well as those who do speak in meetings. Consider diversity in ways of thinking and processing information, perhaps by asking people to write their thoughts first and then speak, or asking people to deliberately take longer to make decisions. There are a number of possibilities but the point is to think about the daily management process and be open for trying new things that may challenge traditional behaviours.

When it comes to performance assessment and reward, people should be judged not only on achieving production targets and sales but also on behavioural aspects of how they achieved those targets, what principles they based their decisions on, what values they demonstrated and how well they enabled a culture of inclusion.

Pay attention to language

It is easy to slip into culturally normal ways of speaking, which often reinforce stereotypes. Be cautious and intentional about what words are chosen to talk about certain groups, and bear in mind what messages they convey.

Be careful about what you turn a blind eye to. By ignoring sexist, racist, homophobic or other comments that demean particular groups (even if they are just jokes), you give a message about what the organization believes is OK. Small things set the tone.

Role model desired behaviours

When senior leaders are aware and open about their own bias and background, and are seen to be actively working to shift these, they give others the inspiration and confidence to do the same. They also show, through their own actions and words, specific ways in which it can be done.

Leading by example is important. Any example of leaders not living up to the declared intended values mitigates the immediate impact of the change. Leaders set the tone for what is encouraged and who is listened to, and they have the ability to show, through their own openness and honesty, how they want employees to uphold the values that are critical to the organization.

Create community

As we showed in the earlier section, diversity alone is not a sufficient aim. Throwing people from different backgrounds together doesn't automatically create positive connections between them. You have to give some thought to the contextual factors that enable different groups to co-exist and co-operate rather than compete and have conflict. A key responsibility of leaders and managers is to create a sense of community.

Vision and purpose

A key part of this is developing a strong shared vision – a common purpose and set of values that all can aspire to together. The Appreciative Inquiry process described in Chapter 15, along with strong communications can enable this. This also contributes to a strong group identity – an organizational or a team identity – that can withstand individual differences and enable people to rely on and trust each other. Creating a vision that is inspirational and aspirational and linked to strategic goals shows that the organization is serious about making diversity and inclusion an inherent part of how they operate.

Most manufacturing and construction companies have a strong 'culture of safety'. This is necessary to maintain a low accident rate and keep workers and customers free from harm. A culture of safety is usually very strong, with well-understood messages and rules about ways of behaving that reduce risk to oneself and others. It is part of the overall vision and incorporated into all activity. Meetings always start with a safety briefing, the role of the fire warden is taken seriously and anyone (at any level) can raise an issue that they see in the interest of safety with no fear. So, if you are passing by and notice a spill, or a poorly stored set of cables, even if it is outside your own area, you have the responsibility and the authority to call out the potential hazard – to speak up – regardless of your role level or area of work. Safety is paramount. People are expected to be responsible and are empowered to take action in the service of a safety culture.

Can a culture of inclusion operate in the same way?

When the principle of inclusion becomes core to organizational identity (like the principle of safety in the above example), it becomes part of normal operating procedure. Anyone, at any level, can 'speak up' and reinforce the messages. All employees (not just those at the top or those in HR) take it on as a personal responsibility to enforce, role-model and uphold the value of inclusion.

Shared and similar sense of belonging

All members of the group need to feel like they belong and fit in here. They need to believe they are entitled to be there and that they are valued, regardless of and *for* the difference they bring in terms of background, experience and perspective. No one group should feel more entitled or more valued just because of their race, class, age, gender, background, accent, education or any other characteristics. One strong leader we spoke to refers to the team as 'family'. This implies giving and receiving support, 'having your back' and being loyal.

Equal opportunities

It is key that not only do all members of the group believe they have similar opportunities to succeed if they put in the effort required. Employees need to have faith that the organization will be fair and that their input will be recognized and rewarded, otherwise it hampers performance and effectiveness. An Equal Opportunities statement is not enough. This can only be achieved by ensuring true transparency in talent management processes and a concerted effort to reduce the impact of bias on how people are selected, treated, judged and rewarded.

Co-operation not competition

Teams across the organization need to see each other not as competitors but as partners working towards a common goal. Very often, a climate of internal competition can create unhealthy working patterns where the emphasis is on visible individual or small team output rather than what is best for the organization as a whole. Similarly, if different groups (genders, races, ages, etc.) are to work effectively together, intergroup competition needs to be eliminated. Strong and positive relationships between individuals within the group are fostered when there is no perceived threat or competition for scarce resources and people are rewarded for collaboration not for achieving selfish targets.

A new leader of a team identified that one of the issues facing the team and the wider organization was having a rigid hierarchy. People were not expected to speak to people above their pay grade, without some degree of formality or by invitation. The head of the department had an office into which typically only their direct reports entered and only when invited. Communication was typically downwards and given by the head to managers, who then communicated it to their supervisors, who then communicated to their teams. There was a culture of fear, that is, if you did 'step out of line' by speaking outside of the hierarchy, then things could go bad for you – bad meant lack of promotions, bad year end review which meant impact on discretionary pay, and so on.

We ran an Appreciative Inquiry intervention in this organization and what emerged as a collective vision for the future was more free flow of information. People recanted themes of historic leaders who had stood out for speaking directly to their teams, cutting hierarchy and having a more open and equal culture.

As a result of this, small changes were made. We held cross-functional and cross-level forums, with no agenda, just an opportunity for people to ask questions and discuss a range of topics openly. The door of the head's office was intentionally left open more frequently. The head started to share information more directly with the wider team together and not through a cascade. Team members were invited into the head's office and asked their opinion. The phrase 'speak up culture' was repeated often, as something positive. People were initially suspicious and hesitant. They started to 'test' (with some caution) if the leader was serious about this change.

Slowly, these actions started becoming more and more normal and consistent. Managers and supervisors replicated the leader's approach. Over time, a new culture was created through consistent, small micro-behaviours that set the tone and collectively changed a fundamental way of working.

Summary

Leadership and behaviour are inter-connected and key to creating change in the context of culture and diversity. However, change does not take place in only a top-down manner, and leadership development is not something that should be focused solely on the few senior people at the top of organizations. The way we work now is more networked and less hierarchical. Leadership, as a quality, is needed at all levels and across the organization, and leadership needs to be emergent, distributed and situational. Leaders need to be self-aware, adaptive, reflective, analytic, humble and empathic, and they need to lead by example to set the tone for the kind of behaviour that is desired.

By being open and honest, leaders can facilitate a safe, speak-up culture where people can have meaningful conversations about diversity and difference without fear of reprisal. Bias needs to be addressed head on and without blame, by helping people identify and challenge stereotypical thinking and expand their cognitive awareness. Leaders need to create a sense of community where different groups are motivated to collaborate in striving towards a shared vision.

---

[1] Western, S. (2013). *Leadership: A Critical Text*. Sage.

[2] Hersey, P., & Blanchard, K. H. (1969). *Management of organizational behavior*. Englewood Cliffs, NJ: Prentice-Hall.

[3] Greenleaf, R. K. (2008). *The Servant as Leader*. Greenleaf Center for Servant Leadership. Indiana, USA.

Governance, process and metrics

The final phases of the approach cover the practical aspects of how we establish inclusive practices across the organization. This is about getting small, daily practices embedded in the normal functioning of the organization at different levels and enforcing these behaviours until they become normalized business-as-usual. This is done through three aspects:

➤ establishing governance (i.e. activity that co-ordinates the work),
➤ changing processes (both HR and general business processes) and
➤ continuous measurement (metrics).

We cover these three phases in a single chapter because they are highly inter-connected and this is work that many organizations already do in the area of Diversity & Inclusion.

The focus here is to ensure there is congruence across the different aspects of organizational functioning. Creating congruence means that the vision and values actually drive process and practice on a day-to-day basis in different areas of organizational design: people, buildings, products, machines, process, policy, etc. Diversity does not sit apart as a separate function or department or as a separate agenda. It needs to become embedded into *the way that things are done* in the organization.

To explain this, we draw on Galbraith's STAR model.[1] This is of the most holistic approaches to understanding organizations and was developed by Jay Galbraith in the 1960s. It is referred to as the STAR model because it has five 'spokes':

➤ Strategy
➤ Structure
➤ Processes
➤ Reward
➤ People

This is a simple and effective way to think about organizational functioning. Each organization will have its own unique formula for success, but regardless of industry or aims, these five key aspects need to be aligned for an organization to work effectively. Strategy refers to the overall direction or purpose of the organization. Structure refers to the 'shape' of an organization, and how people and power are located. Processes are about information flow and technology. Reward refers to how people are paid and incentivized. People refers to HR policies that personally affect employees.

The five elements are connected with each other and any organizational change effort needs to take them all into account. Many change efforts fail because they focus on only one or two aspects, without paying heed to the others. For example, when re-structuring an organization, you not only need to look at organizational charts and the hierarchy, you also need to take into account the logistical processes that will change as a result (recruitment, line management, IT, office locations), the reward programmes that need to be adapted in line with new roles (reward structures, bonuses, pay grades), how the new structure might impact people personally (redundancies) and how the new structure helps the overall direction of the company. All these aspects must be aligned with each other and act in conjunction in order to create a sustainable and smooth change. The five aspects together form a framework that can be used for organizational design, for decision-making and for understanding and changing culture.

When these aspects work in harmony with each other, they reinforce and enable each other. When they are not in unison, time is spent by the organization in mis-direction and potentially chaos. Using this model as a basis for this final stage of the culture change process means seeing how inclusive practice is reflected and reinforced through each element. In many organizations, the aspects are implemented independently, resulting in disparate initiatives. Practices such as flexible working policies, parental leave and women's leadership programmes are introduced in insolation without the support of a cohesive strategy. As such, their impact is minimized or negligible as a method of sustainable or significant change for the organization.

This chapter looks at the final three phases of the approach in the context of holistic organizational design. It outlines the requirements of governance, process and metrics and makes the link with strategy and structure. This ensures that inclusion is not set apart from but aligned with the overall business strategy, and it is incorporated into business as usual.

Holistic organizational design

Frameworks such as the STAR model provide guidance for diagnosis as well as action because they remind us to pay attention to the different inter-related aspects of organizational design. Strong cultures are created through the different aspects working in harmony. Below is an example.

Example of a culture of 'risk-management' through STAR model

A defining principle for one financial services organization was risk management. This was seen to be a key strength by its founders, and a quality which differentiated it from many other financial services organizations, who, for example, may have paid greater emphasis on growth or shareholder return. This characteristic was seen to be responsible for its longevity and resilience, and had become critical to the brand identity. Various aspects of organizational practice reflected this:

Strategy: Risk management was written into strategic objectives. Internal control systems helped calculate the nature and extent of the risk required to achieve strategic objectives. Annual planning was presented with analysis of the risk inherent in every decision.

People: In recruiting new employees, those showing characteristics such as 'solidity' and having a cautious approach were preferred. The hiring process was slow because there were multiple checks of all documents and references. Appointments to senior levels required the formal approval of committees and additional vetting. Risk management training was mandatory for all employees and it was detailed and frequent.

Structure: Risk managers were part of every business team. A Head of Risk sat as part of the Executive Board as an advisor to the Chief Executive. Committees existed to make cross business/functional decisions. Meetings were noted and recorded so decisions could be reviewed. Operating standards were clear, as were levels of delegated authority.

Processes: There was a formal, documented policy in place for every business process. Every department was required to undergo risk assessments on an annual basis and audits were done randomly and on a cyclical basis to ensure that policy was documented and followed within each department. Every decision required duplicate and hierarchical signatures and there was little flexibility or discretion allowed in most process.

Reward: Managers who created risk for the organization were required to 'appear' in front of committees to explain their decisions, and they were penalized through reduction of variable pay. The successful passing of audits, reading policy and evidence of documentation of the measurement and management of risk formed part of the explicit (and rewarded) expectation of every department head.

The above example is not intended to imply that this is the sort of culture that is required for every organization or for every financial services organization. In this case, the concept of risk management was seen to be core and critical for that organization because of its history, position and perspective, and this was how it was implemented across the different aspects of its design, creating a very strong culture that focused heavily on risk.

The effect of this was that it created a strong general pattern of risk avoidance. Individuals followed the process and avoided risk. Spontaneity, creativity, acting on instinct, following through on ideas, 80:20 solutions and strong individual contribution was not common. This worked for this organization as behaviours and processes were all in service of the larger strategic aims. All of this gave the organization a character and the intended competitive advantage. For another organization, where perhaps the focus needs to be on innovation or design, such a culture might be ineffective and actually create an impediment to competitiveness by making processes slower and restrictive. This is why it is crucial to examine the particular context and overall strategic direction of your organization and understand how different process and practical elements should be aligned with it.

In considering how to build an inclusive culture, the same care needs to be taken to ensure that initiatives and policies across different organizational areas are intentional and congruent. This is key to achieving sustainable change and the desired culture – by design.

Linking strategy with inclusion

Strategy is the manner in which the organization talks about where it wants to go and why. This is articulated in a vision, mission, objective, goals and priorities. All of this language tells us the direction of the company and implies also what it will not do. The strategy specifically delineates the products or services to be provided, the markets to be served and the value to be offered to the customer. It also specifies sources of competitive advantage.

Strategy is the first key consideration because all of the other components will be aligned with it. A good strategy is one that is clear, well-understood, talked about and simple to relate to. In other words, all employees must be able to make the connection between their role and job and the overall strategic direction and aims of the organization.

If we are saying that an 'inclusive culture' is the right answer, then the question that the strategy must answer is why it important right now to have an inclusive culture, in the same way that a financial services organization might need a culture of risk? The following aspects (not exhaustive) of strategy illustrate how inclusion may be relevant to strategy:

Acquisitive growth (e.g. buying another company, merging, joint venture) requires bringing different working styles and cultures together. These attempts often fail because culture clash. An inclusive culture makes all feel involved, and creates a sense of 'one team'.

Organic growth (e.g. focus on service and products to grow customer base, exploring new markets and seizing opportunities for competitive growth) needs a flexible organization that can respond to changes in the environment quickly and adaptively. An inclusive organization has more trust and open dialogue, so people feel included and empowered to make decisions. Diversity allows greater flexibility of working patterns and thinking in the organization, helping it to respond to market conditions with more agility.

Organizational Change (e.g. structural change, new systems, cost reduction) rely on employees being flexible and maintaining confidence and work effort through the change. An inclusive culture ties people together, and creates greater trust.

Innovation (i.e. focus on creating new products to gain an edge in the market), at a basic level, is about generating fresh ideas and implementing them. An innovative organization allows innovation not just in terms of producing 'big' new products but also displaying creativity at the process level. An environment where employees feel respected and included fosters greater sharing of new ideas as well as more openness and creativity.

One perspective that can be leveraged in making the strategic link with this work is taking an employee-centred perspective, like an employee value proposition (EVP). EVP is a term used to collectively articulate what the organization, as an employer, can offer the people who work in it. It includes reward (salary), recognition, social rewards, perks, brand and all aspects that might entice people to join. It is what attracts talented employees and motivates them to stay in the company, ultimately contributing to a stronger and more competitive organization. Inclusion is a key aspect of EVP. It is a 'selling point' to potential employees and enables the organization to attract a wider pool of talent.

In this way, the first step in embedding process change into the culture is to look at strategy and make the link with inclusion.

Once this link is made, it is important to communicate the link and the strategic aims with regard to inclusion clearly. Everyone in the organization needs to be aware of it, remember it and see their work as being aligned with it.

It also needs to be sustainable. The work on culture should be seen as critical enough to transcend the immediate management team and the current leaders of the organization. It needs to be understood and accepted by enough of the core group of the organization to be able to live through management changes.

A common pitfall in diversity work is that it relies on the support of a key senior sponsor or a particularly passionate CEO, and when that person leaves, the work dies out. It is important to consider the legacy beyond current leadership and solidify the foundations of this work in core organizational functioning.

A final consideration is about shared ownership. The department or consultancy doing this work needs to be careful not to become possessive or engage in 'turf wars'. This work spans a wide range of functions and competencies, and it needs to be seen as something the whole organization is engaged in, rather than being an 'HR' initiative. Thus, by linking inclusion with organizational strategy, it becomes something we are all working on together, as part of what we do.

Establishing governance

Governance is about daily activity to co-ordinate work, for example, meetings, committees and reporting mechanisms. To adopt the appropriate governance, we have to understand the structural design at a organizational level, as well as the nuances of how the organization brings groups together to do things, for example, who is in charge of major committees? Do new coordinating mechanisms/special project teams need to be created to drive new focus? What mediums are used to report progress? Governance needs to be carefully chosen based on the current norms as well as the desired culture.

Nearly all change models will suggest that change needs to be led from the top. Senior level sponsorship is certainly critical to potential success. This means the Board/Executive Officers sanction the work and the Chairman/Chief Executive Officer have control of the initiative. One of the issues with this, however, is that by using the existing methods of governance and control in the organization, one is re-enforcing the already existing structures and power. It is therefore important that the work is simultaneously done in multiple places and in multiple ways so that there is shared ownership and also shared leadership that will truly mobilize the change.

Governance and structure

Before establishing governance, we need to understand how the organization is structured, and how power is distributed. Is authority linked with role level, expertise, position or charisma? Who has decision-making power currently, and how does power potentially need to be distributed in order to support the aims of an inclusive culture? Who has to 'sign off' or give permission for this work and how will it be managed? Authority is granted via structure and governance will help to enforce desired behaviours. The governance therefore articulates what the organization considers to be most important to uphold.

We need to consider centralization and de-centralization of authority, as well as how informal and formal networks can be leveraged. Vertical control of decision-making reflects a 'traditional' top-down model of command and control. Decentralized decision-making pushes the power down to teams and people who may be dispersed across the organization and who may be closer to its products, customers and local geographical differences. To understand structure and power, you may need to ask:

- What type of company is this? What do we do here?
- What is most important to the strategy – product, function,

geography?

- Who does the current structure assign power to?
- Where does real power lie?
- Where are things done similarly in a standard way and where is one part of the organization given 'permission' to do things in a different way and why?

The optimal way to organize the structure and way to build in governance will be different for different organizations. Current processes may be a reflection of the organization's unique administrative history and may reflect a national bias as to how work is organized. Organizations may be organized along a functional, product line, customer segment, geography and work-flow processes. In many cases, a hybrid structure or matrix structure, which is a mix of these aspects, emerges. It is important to understand this and work within this structure to get the right approvals to proceed with the work.

Yet, it is also important to challenge the existing structure where it is, by its very nature, counter to the current strategic aims. There is no one ideal structure to aim for. You need to carefully consider the current operating context and strategic aims, and intentionally align structure and governance with this. Some considerations are:

- What is the focus of the organization currently?
- What phase of the work are we in currently, and what is the governance requirement at this phase?
- Where does power lie in the organization, and where can a new aspect of culture be tested and taken to scale quickly?

Human resource processes

Formal HR processes define how people are treated and managed through their 'life cycle' in the organization: from the time they apply for a job, through to when they leave or retire. HR processes are key to Diversity & Inclusion because they define how critical decisions are made about selecting, assessing and promoting people, which are key indicators of inclusion and equality. Examining the processes by which we manage people is critical to understanding how diversity plays out and how it is managed.

Much of the current Diversity and Inclusion work resides in this area. It includes:

- Monitoring metrics (demographics of who is hired, promoted, etc.) and
- Monitoring process (e.g. how interviews are conducted, how performance is assessed).

It also includes

- Implementing new policies and practices (e.g. flexible working, maternity leave) and
- Interventions (e.g. mentoring, training, sponsorship programmes).

While all this work is extremely valuable and relevant, very often, it is not cohesive and not linked with overall strategy, and this is partly why it loses impact.

For example, flexible working is generally viewed as a policy dictated by HR. It is not seen as an aspirational aspect of culture. Therefore, very often, it falls down in practice because it is seen to be a perk for some employees, rather than a norm, and not all local managers may be supportive of it. So, the execution may be patchy and inconsistent and managers may be flexible to the bare minimum extent that is required by law or by the organizational policy, rather than adopting it as a new way of working. In order to become a norm, it needs to be seen as something that is aligned with business goals. Flexibility is not just good for employees, it is good for the organization because it enables it to be more adaptive and agile to external events and customer demands. Work time can be stretched and a wider range of employees can be employed and engaged. Often, there is a cost associated with such interventions or changes (e.g. new technologies to support remote working), so the benefit to the business needs to be articulated as a strategic imperative not as a 'nice to have' or a 'must have' that is dictated by HR.

Similarly, maternity leave is seen to be an exception or adjustment made for some (female) employees, rather than something that is part of the way business is done. If gender diversity is worked into the strategic direction of the company in terms of competitiveness and capability, then maternity (and paternity) leave will be a natural action rather than something that needs to be justified. Currently, paternal leave, absence management, on and off ramping and other such policies are written in the tone of administration and enforcement rather than something that is inspirational and aspirational.

Reducing the impact of bias

Ultimately, the key aim of this phase is to use governance to make HR processes inclusive and free of bias. Bias is not normally obvious or visible, but its impact can be seen in the disparities between different groups represented at different levels in the organization or in rates of promotion of different groups. Bias itself can also be measured, through tests like the Implicit Association Test, at an individual level. Collating results of all employees can give us an idea of what the institutional effect may be, and it also may help to explain certain disparities in representation.

We talked in Chapter 16 about ways in which to address bias at a personal and organizational level by decriminalizing bias, encouraging self-reflection and giving managers training as well as opportunities to widen their perspectives. In addition to this kind of personal work, there are process changes that also help to mitigate the impact of bias. Here are some examples:

- Outlining clear competencies for jobs and ensuring these are specific and job-related and not inadvertently placing any group at a disadvantage
- Recruiting for diversity by targeting particular universities or using a range of media to reach currently under-represented groups
- Using a variety of mediums and publications so that a wider pool of people are reached
- Creating panels to interview and select staff, not leaving it up to the discretion of one person, so that the impact of any one person's bias can be neutralized
- Making sure interview panels are diverse (e.g. have a mix of men and women and people from different backgrounds) to give a more all-round perspective
- Remove information that can cloud judgement where possible, for example, reviewing CVs 'blind', that is, without name or date of birth
- Making talent processes transparent, so all employees can clearly see what they need to do to progress, and it is not left to luck or contacts.

In many companies, senior jobs are not always consistently posted, which leaves room for favouritism and discrimination in terms of who is invited to apply

- Review the process by which performance management decisions are made, for example, by having a 'second opinion' or using 360 feedback
- Review the process by which targets are set and bonuses are awarded. Are these putting all employees on a level playing field? For example, we saw in one organization that when women were going on maternity leave, their sales performance assessment over the year was not taking into account their time on leave. So, if they took six months off, their performance 'rate' was being calculated by dividing their annual performance by 12 not by the 6 actual months that they worked. This put them at a disadvantage compared with colleagues who worked the whole year
- Review managers not only on what they achieve (meeting targets or making sales) but also on how they do their work and how they treat their employees. This can be done using behavioural indicators (designed around inclusive practice) and linking them with performance assessment
- In meetings (particularly where performance of employees is being discussed), appoint one person to play the overt role of 'steward' of the values. This person is given the job and the authority to point out when a decision or a conversation indicates possible bias. For example, they ask for evidence or dismiss generalizations. They highlight when a person's qualities are being discussed in a stereotypical way or when non-job-related factors are influencing a decision. They look out for non-verbal behaviours that can create micro-inequities
- During on-boarding, new employees can undergo a 'rite of passage', which includes an active and overt commitment to the value of inclusion, as a condition for joining the organization.
- Consider how a typical work day is structured. Is there any 'down time' for employees? Is there any time and space for them to engage the 'default networks' in their brains, which is crucial for imagination, innovation and empathy?
- Consider workload and stress levels. People are much more likely to fall back on cognitive 'shortcuts' and make biased decisions when they are under pressure or short of time.

Business processes and the link with inclusion

Processes exist and need to be considered, not only in HR, but across all functions in the organization. This includes *how we do* things every day: from how team meetings are run and how local sales staff are incentivized, to business reporting and risk management. All these minor and major processes ultimately drive and enforce a particular culture.

Core ways of doing business often reflect historical biases and some of these may be worth re-considering. For example:

– What time of day and what days of the week are meetings generally held? Who is this time best suited to? Who is it least suited to? Are there certain people who may struggle to attend at these times?
– How are decisions made at a team level? Who is involved in making the decisions? When and where are the decisions made? Who is included and who is excluded from this process and why?
– Who is the customer, and what are their needs? Do we really understand the segment of the population who is buying our products and services? What are the demographics and how have they changed?
– How are organizational charts drawn? What shape do they normally take and what does this indicate in terms of hierarchy and power? Are there other ways to draw them?
– Where do people normally work? Are they based at an office or site or can they work from anywhere? Why is it like that, and what are the advantages and disadvantages? Is there an alternative?
– When do people normally work? Is it between certain times or round the clock? Do employees have fixed hours or flexible hours? What are the advantages and disadvantages of how it is, and is there an alternative?
– What is the primary business language? Does it have to be that way? What is the impact on local offices in different parts of the world?

The HR or OD team, or consultancy working on culture, may not be in a position to change core business processes. This needs to come from the business process owner, and this is why it is so important that this work is seen to be something the whole organization is involved in together, so all process owners take responsibility for their contribution to it. All business and functional processes, not just HR, need to and can be aligned with cultural values and goals. Disconnects between the desired values and how things are done in any part of the business impedes the process of culture change and inclusion.

Metrics and monitoring

The most basic and widespread Diversity and Inclusion practice, monitoring, refers to the collection and analysis of demographic data about employees (e.g. age, gender and ethnicity). In the most obvious sense, monitoring demographic data tells you how diverse a group of people is because it lists the percentage who fall into each of the measured categories. The goal of workforce monitoring is to identify where discrepancies exist in terms of representation (when compared to the relevant wider population). For example, assuming the population is about 50 per cent female, if a certain organization has only 20 per cent female staff, it points to the existence of some kind of barrier to gender equality when it comes to recruitment. The reasons for this may be internal to the organization (e.g. biases in selection, recruiting from limited pools, female-unfriendly policies) or external (e.g. a male-dominated industry, cultural gender roles). Usually, of course, there are a variety of reasons. Monitoring data often form the starting point of any diversity initiative because these help us identify a problem to target.

Ideally, monitoring should be done at different levels (e.g. the organization may well have 50 per cent of female staff overall, but it might be 70 per cent at junior levels and 10 per cent at senior levels – and this points to a problem with selective attrition or bias in promotion). Monitoring should also be done across different areas in an organization (different departments and geographies) and at different stages in the employee life cycle – at selection (including who applies, who is shortlisted and who is finally selected), promotions and exiting the organization (resignations, redundancies and dismissals), including critical junctures such as performance management, training opportunities and employee grievances.

Often, monitoring is done in a 'flat' way: organizations only look at the static data of who currently is employed in the organization rather than also looking at the dynamic data of who enters, leaves and thrives in the organization. Is there a pattern in who gets assigned to certain types of clients/projects, who gets sent on training courses or who gets their leave requests granted? What are the differences in employee engagement across different groups, or the differences in reasons for leaving (in exit questionnaires)? It is these data that really help to uncover not just who is in the organization but what their employee experience is like compared to others. This is where monitoring data can be really helpful to uncover some of the more detailed and subtle differences in employee experience which eventually contribute to an unequal environment and a lack of diversity.

Here is a range of options for what can be measured to help shed light on inclusion and diversity, and this extends far beyond simple monitoring of demographics.

- Employee profile (percentage of different groups, at different levels, across function and geography)
- At what level does the profile change? For example, is there a particular salary grade where the percentage of women drops? Do we understand why this is the case?
- Are there certain parts of the business where the profile is different from the overall profile? For example, are there certain departments that are female- or male-dominated, or certain levels that have predominantly one ethnicity or educational background? Do we know why this is the case and how is it justified?
- Employee segmentation into 'types' to understand unique needs of different segments of the population (segments are groupings that are based on multiple factors, such as age, gender, country and type of work, rather than just using a singular axis of difference).
- Profile of who applies, who gets invited to interview and who gets selected.
- Performance assessment scores of different groups at different levels.
- Rates of promotion of different groups at different levels and in different departments/geographies.
- Profile of who gets particular types of assignments (e.g. graduate programmes, international assignments, rotations).
- Profile of who gets particular types of allowances (e.g. extended leave, sabbaticals).
- Turnover rates of different groups of employees at different levels.

- What percentage of the workforce have the option to work from home? And what percentage actually work from home, at least sometimes? Are there any demographic or other differences here (e.g. manager vs. non-manager)?
- What percentage of people have fixed versus flexible hours? Are there any demographic or other differences here (e.g. manager vs. non-manager)?
- Employee engagement scores for different groups. Are there any differences by gender, age, ethnicity, location, and so on?
- Grievances or complaints. Are there differences by demographics or types of employees?

In addition, there are indicators that can be used to measure aspects of the culture, specifically, inclusion. For example, questions can be asked in an employee survey to measure perception of whether:

- The organization is seen to be fair/inclusive
- Managers are seen to be fair/inclusive
- The talent management process is understood
- People feel like they have the opportunity to progress here
- People from different background feel included
- Different ideas are welcomed/difference is embraced
- There is pressure to conform or agree with others
- People feel able to 'speak up' and voice their opinions
- People feel personally valued and appreciated for their difference
- People feel they are treated equally

There is a wide range of such indicators and they can be designed to align with the stated goals around inclusion and worded in a way that fits the organization.

Answers to questions like the above should be analysed by the different groups to understand differences in employee experience and variation in how people view the organization from within.

It is important to ask these questions – not just to get numerical scores but to get a deeper understanding of what sits behind the numbers and what story it tells us about the processes at play in the organization.

Despite the fact that monitoring is fundamental to diversity management, one of the biggest issues with it is that often organizations get stuck on the numbers and don't get 'beyond the bean-counting' to understand why discrepancies exist and how they can be addressed. The numbers are only a starting point, a 'status check'. The real work of Diversity and Inclusion is understanding why and making appropriate cultural changes. Often, token gestures are implemented to 'fix' specific discrepancies and the focus remains on minute movements in the numbers (rather than the surrounding context). If the percentage of employees with a disability at role level X moved from 2 to 2.3 this year, what does that mean in real terms? Is the change important or significant in the current climate? What other changes have taken place this year? How has the *experience* of having a disability in this organization changed this year?

Another very common problem with monitoring is lack of data. In the vast majority of organizations, for example, there are just too few females or ethnic minorities or openly gay employees at the senior-most level to have any sensible discussion about percentages. Yet, often organizations get fixated on meaningless percentages (e.g. examining percentage of females in a board of ten members) as there is nothing else to 'hold on to'. They get bogged down with the statistics (e.g. a change of 10 per cent sounds large, but of course it only represents one person if the size of the group is 10) rather than taking a different approach – for example, qualitative enquiry.

In other situations, data doesn't exist because it is not collected (e.g. on faith or sexual orientation) due to legal or cultural reasons in certain countries, because insufficient number of employees answered the question, or because the question doesn't currently exist in the employee database. In such cases, organizations often become paralysed because there is no 'evidence base' for them to work from, and the issues remain unaddressed. Many organizations only really hold sufficient data on age and gender, and these become the focus of diversity efforts, and other realms of difference receive less or no attention.

It is crucial to monitor employee statistics and to do so rigorously, but it is also important to be able to move beyond the numbers. Reliance on numbers alone prevents more dynamic action and big change because we become focused only on what we can easily measure and we exhaust our resources on analysis rather than action. It is also important to monitor not just 'flat' demographics but also look at a wide range of information (qualitative and quantitative) to help paint a fuller picture of what its like to work here and how inclusive the organization is.

Quotas and targets

In November 2012, the European Commission (EC) put forward legislation that aimed to boost the percentage of women non-executive directors on the boards of big listed companies, from 15 per cent to 40 per cent by 2020. This has set off a period of heated debate within governments and the business community across Europe, about the value of setting targets, and the need for establishing quotas for women in the workplace. While quotas dictate a compulsory minimum, targets indicate an aspiration. Targets are a percentage that a company promises to, and demonstrates that it is, working towards. There are no harsh penalties for not achieving targets, but the company may be responsible for explaining what measures were taken, and why targets have not been met.

On the one hand, it is acknowledged that quotas can create a step-change by forcing organizations into taking action immediately. It is a drastic measure but one that may be needed following slow progress to date. On the other hand, it is a 'band-aid' solution in some ways because it doesn't really get to the heart of the problem. One of the reasons for lack of female representation at the top is because females are lacking in the 'talent pipeline'. More may be gained from focusing on women at lower ranks, and finding ways in which they can become qualified and experienced enough to apply for and inherit the senior-most roles. Otherwise, even if women are appointed into senior roles, once they leave or retire, there will be no females to take their place, and the situation will go back to where it was. The real issue of gender doesn't lie at the top of organizations but somewhere in the middle, where women between the ages of 25 and 35 are choosing to leave the workforce in order to have children. This is where there is an attrition problem in many organizations, and if this was addressed, the female 'pipeline' to the senior roles would no longer be leaking!

There is also a realistic fear that by setting compulsory quotas, the women who do get appointed will be viewed as less qualified by their male peers because the assumption will be that they got promoted because of their gender and not their talent. Many women are therefore against it. The argument, however, is that no smaller measure has really been able to address this deeply rooted and unyielding inequality and a quota may be the only way to jump start the change.

Some private organizations have proactively decided to set quotas in order to enhance gender or racial diversity within their employee or user base, because they see this as a necessary step to create the change that is needed. For example, Sky Television in the UK announced recently that by the end of 2015, all their original commissions will have at least one (out of six) senior production executive, and at least 20 per cent of writers (in team-written shows), from Black, Asian or minority ethnic backgrounds. By doing this, they hope not only to make the industry more open to people from these (currently under-represented) backgrounds, but also to ensure that their teams will be best placed to create programmes that reflect the perspectives of their ethnically diverse audience. They have also committed to showing people from Black, Asian or minority ethnic backgrounds in at least 20 per cent of significant on-screen roles on all new shows, for all genres. Their Director of Entertainment Channels, Stuart Murphy, says 'Black, Asian or minority ethnic networks have told us pretty clearly that they don't want more training schemes – they want a break'.[2]

The reason quotas and targets are set is to indicate an intention, a direction and a commitment to action. Compulsory quotas (rather than aspirational targets) make this commitment more loudly and compel organizations to take immediate action. However, it is essential that along with setting a target or quota, work is done to address the underlying reasons for representational disparity: not only the talent pipeline, but also the culture, the context and the ways in which men, women, ethnic minorities and everyone else experience the environment and what motivates them to join, stay and leave.

There are pros and cons, and many risks to consider when setting a quota or a target. Such an action needs to be aligned with organizational culture and readiness, and it needs to fit within a wider strategic plan. For some organizations, for example, nothing really happens without specific goals being articulated, so setting targets becomes necessary. For others, targets may be seen as unmeritocratic and counter-cultural and there may be too much backlash. Those women or minority candidates who are appointed may face and adverse reaction from colleagues who attribute their promotion to quotas rather than ability. Sometimes, selected candidates face so much pressure from bias and underlying hostility that it ultimately affects their performance and then the failure of the individual is seen to be a failure of that whole group to hold positions at that level. This then becomes a precedent for organizations to use when they say 'we tried' a diverse/female/young/ different candidate and 'it didn't work'.

Sometimes managers and leaders say there is a realistic difficulty to find qualified, diverse candidates because certain groups are generally under-represented at lower levels or in the industry as a whole – so the issue is that there aren't enough diverse candidates in the pipeline, for example, women in engineering schools, or minorities in senior management. This may be true on the surface when you look at the statistics, however, 'lack of candidates' is often an excuse, and the real issue is that the organization is not looking in the right places or trying hard enough or being creative enough about how they attract a diverse pool of applicants. If this is the case, then you will need to address the perception first and demonstrate how the organization can look more widely to overcome the problem, before setting quotas and targets that may be seen as impossible. You will need to decide when and how to challenge the thinking and at what stage in the process targets will be more effective.

You need to consider the current climate in the organization and in society more widely and take into account how far along the journey towards inclusion an organization is, and whether the timing is right for the interventions you choose.

Summary

This section explains the final three phases of building an inclusive culture.

Recommendations are framed around a model of organizational design, the STAR model, where the key is to ensure there is congruence between strategy, process, people, reward and metrics. Diversity & Inclusion should not sit separately from business; it should be core to how things are done, and aligned with the overall strategy. It should be part of process (both HR processes and wider business processes), and governance should be in place to support and enforce this in a way that is aligned with the desired culture and strategy.

Metrics are needed as a way to measure progress. At a basic level, this refers to monitoring demographic profiles of employees at different levels and in different parts of the business. There are a wide range of more dynamic measures that can be employed to help understand the cultural aspects of inclusion and highlight discrepancies in employee experience.

These final stages are the so-called 'hard' aspects of culture, which define the way that things are done every day. It is critical to pay attention to the big and the small decisions, the major and minor processes and the HR as well as wider business activity, to ensure that inclusive practices become truly embedded into the normal day-to-day functioning across the organization.

---

[1] Kates, A., & Galbraith, J. R. (2010). *Designing Your Organization: Using the STAR Model to Solve 5 Critical Design Challenges*. John Wiley & Sons, USA.

[2] http://corporate.sky.com/skyviews/sky/increasing_diversity_across_sky_entertainment_channels, Retrieved 1 October 2014.

Conclusion

Chapter 18

Final thoughts

On a hot afternoon in March 1993, I sat in my school hall in Mumbai (then Bombay), writing the final exam of my tenth year. It was a monumental occasion, the last day of school – ever. For all of us in that room, the day marked a transition to the next stage of life, and we were brimming with excitement about the parties we had planned for that evening and the plans we had for college and life after school.

Suddenly we heard a loud bang. Teachers pacified us by saying it was nothing to worry about, some electrical fault perhaps, and encouraged us to keep our heads down and keep writing.

In fact, it was far from nothing. Across the city, bombs were going off. Outside the exam hall, riots had broken out – apparently between Hindus and Muslims. While we were safely cocooned in the school walls for the few hours that followed, just outside our gates, people were fighting, stabbing and killing each other. I still recall one parent walking through the gates, crying desperately as she had fought the mobs to make it into the school to pick up her son. She was covered in blood, but luckily unharmed.

I recall feeling overwhelmed, confused and scared. As a young teenager, it made no sense to me that people were fighting about religion. Surely, no religion really preaches violence and no God would want to see this kind of needless pain and suffering. How could this be justified? I became sure that what these people were fighting about couldn't really be religion. Whether we say it is about religion, or race, or territory, ultimately, it comes down to difference, identity and power.

We remain somewhat naïve in our quest for an answer to this: is there no better way for us to deal with our differences? Shall we accept the conflicts we repeatedly see occurring across the world, and just keep our heads down?

This book is about dealing with diversity in organizations.

The work done in Diversity and Inclusion departments may seem far removed from such larger issues facing humanity. And in many ways, of course it is. Those issues are complex and confounded by strong ideas about politics, economics, geography and history. We are not pretending that an HR manager or an OD consultant can stop world wars or save the planet. However, we are saying that there is a significant role that organizations – especially large multinational organizations – can and do play in shaping how we live and think. Organizations can be a starting point, a beacon for the rest of society and an important harbinger of change in the communities they serve.

Explicitly or implicitly, organizations serve society, whether they are public or private, local or international. For organizations with a clearly 'social' purpose (such as local government, central government, non-governmental organizations or charities), this is obvious in their stated aims. Private organizations also serve society: through the products they create (which are consumed or used by the public), the perceptions, habits or lifestyles they may change, the economies and communities they support and the people they employ.

Like individuals, organizations are citizens of the world, playing a part in reflecting and shaping society. Organizations influence how we think and act at many levels – whether it is as shareholders, consumers, employees or members of the public.

Large global organizations are a microcosm of the globalized world we live in and they have the power (sometimes more so than governments and community organizations) to influence society through their impact on the economy, trade, environment, consumers and politics.

At the time of writing this book, some interesting examples of government vs. corporate emerged in the United States. The State of Indiana (among others) passed legislation to ensure religious freedom. This sought to protect the rights of merchants to *not serve* individuals whose lifestyle (homosexuality, for example) offended their religious beliefs. The passing of the legislation was met with significant public opposition from some 'celebrity' CEOs and corporate public relations teams who felt this new law violated the rights and dignity of gay people. They indicated that they would have to reconsider investment in the State and stopped using the State to hold conferences, business meetings etc. Within the State locally the decision by the state government was met with opposition from the chambers of commerce, tourism and other business leaders. The reaction from the business leaders threatened the short and medium term financial stability and they feared the negative exposure. As a result of this attention and pressure from the corporate world, the legislation was overturned within weeks. This demonstrates the ability of business leaders to set the tone for what they deem acceptable in society and create consequences for going against corporate/societal common values.

Organizations also have the potential to impose a set of required values and ways of working on their employees, which go beyond legislation. They can enforce these values through setting internal standards and making it clear what behaviours are unacceptable. For example, in many organizations, people make sexist, racist or homophobic remarks, which are ignored or laughed off. While these may not be against the law, they dilute the work of creating an inclusive culture. People should know that regardless of how senior, competent or popular they are, words and actions that go against the values will not be tolerated, and that they need to either change their mindset and behaviour, or leave the organization. Organizations cannot function as democracies: it is an apparent contradiction, but often necessary, that in pursuing 'inclusion', the organization will sometimes need to 'exclude' those who do not conform to the desired culture, even at the cost of losing talent. This must, of course, be balanced with the need to maintain equality and personal freedom, and not becoming totalitarian.

Many technology giants from California's Silicon Valley, including Cisco, HP, Microsoft and Intel, are now setting up subsidiaries in the West Bank to leverage the world-class technological talent and entrepreneurship available among Israelis and Palestinians. The West Bank now has about 300 IT firms operating in the region.[1]

There is a huge opportunity here for multinational companies to affect positive change in local communities. An international company can impose a culture of inclusion and mutual respect, showing no tolerance for religious conflict or discrimination in the workplace, which is more than a government may be able to impose in the region. These companies provide an environment where people from different backgrounds are required to cooperate and work effectively together in developing and launching a new product to the world market. People are encouraged to feel part of the global tech giant culture and to become proud of the product and their common association with the brand.

Socially, the work alleviates hardship in some communities and brings employment, enabling payment for health and education. This gives people the breathing space to focus on work, products, software, technology, their common interests and their commercial and inclusive success, rather than politics, competition for resources or divisiveness, which could close the campus. It restores a nobility to those who have been excluded from workplaces, that brings meaning to their lives beyond disenfranchisement.

The corporation thus gives people the position and place to bridge difference and to practice living in a culture of cooperative endeavour. It is not hard to see how this might translate back into the wider community. The chance to work together, to prove worth and to have meaning through work leads to a less disenfranchised society. The private sector plays a significant role in affecting public life and attitude in a positive way through inclusive practices in this way.

It is easy to feel powerless or overwhelmed when facing something as big as 'culture' and to resort, instead, to simple, quick 'fixes'.

Yet, working on culture is critical. There is no point putting in place a new flexible working policy if the organizational culture doesn't support it, and there is no point setting quotas for women without addressing how well women are set up to succeed in society. We have to be intentional about culture – specifically, intentional about creating an inclusive culture. We can't afford to ignore culture or leave it to chance, because if we do, we run the risk of replicating social inequalities and pitfalls, repeating history or allowing prevailing power structures to dictate how things are done.

We need to purposefully create a culture of equality, respect and inclusion, where our differences are not seen as a problem but as a competitive advantage: a quality that can be leveraged to enhance decision-making, problem-solving, creativity and innovation.

Building or changing culture is not an easy task, and it cannot be tackled by simple 'quick-fixes'. Those who initiate this type of work may not see things change immediately. Yes, some numbers may shift, and small wins must be celebrated, but the process of shifting mindset and culture is a long-term process that evolves slowly.

It starts with commitment: a strong set of values – not just a Corporate Vision or an Equal Opportunities Statement published on the website – but a genuine commitment to the aims of inclusion and to the role of the organization as a global citizen. This goes beyond ensuring an ethical supply chain, or good public relations activity for fear of brand erosion on social media. This is about the organization making a conscious choice to uphold the value of inclusion and to being willing to make a public stand and use their power to effect positive change in society.

The Diversity and Inclusion strategy must be congruent with the overall strategy of the organization, as well as the structure, the operating context and the wider social context. This should align with the purpose of the organization and with shareholders, as well as customers, employees and the wider society. The Diversity and Inclusion agenda should be central to the organizational strategy, not an add-on, and not something that is based in a particular philosophy or politic that may not be shared by all in the organization (or even all in the core group of the organization) or that may not survive a change in leadership.

Systems and processes then need to be aligned with the aim, and designed in a way that allows employees to speak up! 'Principled organizational dissent' or protest against injustice within or by the organization can ultimately be in the best interests of the organization and wider society. It allows the organization to self-regulate before any government, pressure group or the media force the organization to make changes. It also facilitates in employees, a sense of civic responsibility, compliance and principled behaviour, even when unsupervised, as they are aligned with the values and they are accountable. This acts as a safeguard for the management and shareholders and it enables employees to be part of something they believe in and are allowed to defend.

Ultimately, this work comes down to *empathy*. This means not just tolerating, but appreciating diversity and difference, and fostering an understanding of other people and perspectives. It has to start within the organization's own walls. It would be disingenuous for an organization to profess good global citizenship if it cannot practice the same behaviour within itself, and towards it's own employees. This goes back to the 'Golden Rule' of treating others with the same degree of acceptance and respect that you would want them to treat you with.

Whatever the stated purpose of organizations (private, public or third sector), they all have the responsibility to pursue their goals in a way that maximizes quality, effectiveness, sustainability and ethics. Diversity & Inclusion is a necessary aspect of this aim. Creating equality of access and opportunity is not only the right thing to do; it is also the necessary and obvious thing to do in today's world. We do not need to extensively research and write yet another business case document to demonstrate the impact of Diversity and Inclusion on success. Diversity & Inclusion is, by definition, a natural aspect of organizational functioning in a diverse world. Having an inclusive culture, where different perspectives are welcomed and valued, and where people are competent to work across difference, enables richer problem-solving and innovation, and ultimately, greater relevance and survival in the diverse context in which we all operate. It serves the interests of our employees, customers, shareholders and societies.

You have a choice

It is not just the leaders of large organizations who have the power to change things. We entrust much of this work to those we place in positions of power. Yet, we all have a choice and we all hold *some* power to create change, however big or small. All change starts somewhere.

Back in 1993, I took the advice of my schoolteacher and kept my head down and kept writing. Today, we invite you to stop and look up, and think consciously about how we can work across our perceived differences in a positive way, rather than allowing difference to destroy us.

We need to work together, with patience and courage – no matter what type of organization we work in or for – to identify and minimize bias and unfairness at an individual and systemic level, to challenge our own cultural assumptions, to foster cross-cultural competence, to build greater empathy and cooperation, and to proactively create an environment that is effective, ethical, equal and inclusive: where everyone can survive and thrive and work together on the journey towards making the world a better place to live.

---

[1] http://www.economist.com/blogs/schumpeter/2014/02/it-west-bank, Retrieved 25 April 2015.

Further Reading

Cooperrider, D., Whitney, D. D., & Stavros, J. M. (2008). *The appreciative inquiry handbook: For leaders of change*. Berrett-Koehler Publishers. USA.

Gladwell, M. (2005). *Blink: The Power of Thinking Without Thinking*. Back Bay Books. New York, NY.

Kahneman, D. (2011). *Thinking, Fast and Slow*. Penguin Books. London.

Kandola, B. (2009). *The Value of Difference: Eliminating Bias in Organisations*. Pearn Kandola Publishing. Oxford.

Kates, A., & Galbraith, J. R. (2010). *Designing Your Organization: Using the STAR Model to Solve 5 Critical Design Challenges*. John Wiley & Sons. USA.

Kleiner, A. (2003). *Who Really Matters: The Core Group Theory of Power, Privilege, and Success*. Random House. USA.

Schein, E. H. (2010). *Organizational culture and leadership* (Vol. 2). John Wiley & Sons. USA.

Schwartz, J., & Gladding, R. (2011). *You Are Not Your Brain: The 4-Step Solution for Changing Bad Habits, Ending Unhealthy Thinking, and Taking Control of Your Life*. Penguin.

Tajfel, H. (2010). *Social identity and intergroup relations*. Cambridge University Press.

Trompenaars, F., Hampden-Turner, C. (1997). *Riding the Waves of Culture: Understanding Cultural Diversity in Business*. Nicholas Brealey Publishing. London.

Western, S. (2013). *Leadership: A Critical Text*.

Index

Note: The locators followed by 'b' and 'n' refer to boxes and notes